100+ IDEAS FOR TEACHING CITIZENSHIP

CONTINUUM ONE HUNDREDS SERIES

100 Ideas for Teaching Citizenship, Ian Davies

100 Ideas for Teaching Creativity, Stephen Bowkett

100 Ideas for Teaching Religious Education, Cavan Wood

100 Ideas for Teaching Thinking Skills, Stephen Bowkett

100+ IDEAS FOR TEACHING CITIZENSHIP

Ian Davies

Continuum One Hundreds

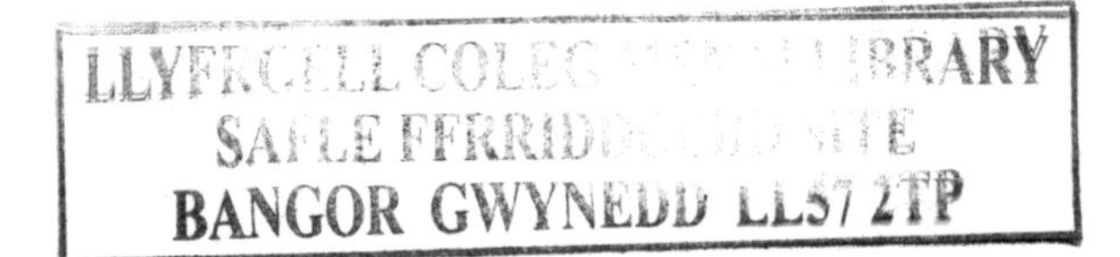

Continuum International Publishing Group

The Tower Building
11 York Road
London, SE1 7NX

80 Maiden Lane
Suite 704, New York
NY 10038

www.continuumbooks.com

British Library Cataloguing-in-Publication Data
A catalogue record for this book is available from the British Library.

ISBN: 978-1-4411-8528-0 (paperback)

Library of Congress Cataloging-in-Publication Data
Davies, Ian, 1957-
100+ ideas for teaching citizenship / Ian Davies.
p. cm.
ISBN: 978-1-4411-8528-0 – ISBN: 978-1-4411-8371-2 – ISBN: 978-1-4411-9294-3 1. Citizenship–Study and teaching. I. Title. II. Title: One hundred plus ideas for teaching citizenship.

LC1091.D278 2011
370.11'50941–dc22 2010045955

Typeset by Newgen Imaging Systems Pvt Ltd, Chennai, India
Printed and bound in India

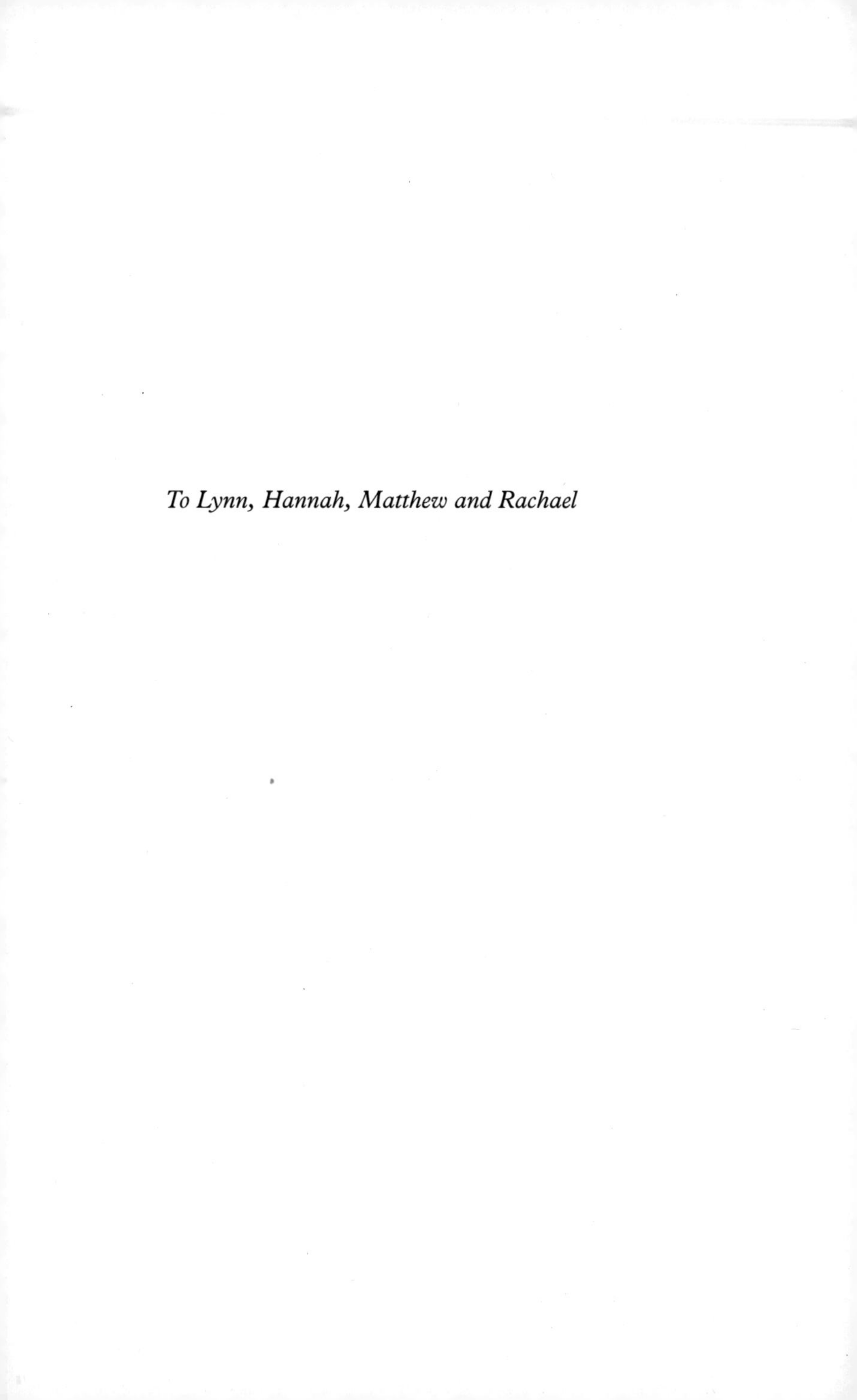

To Lynn, Hannah, Matthew and Rachael

CONTENTS

SECTION 10 **What Can I Do to Set Up a Mock Election?**

SECTION 11 **Citizenship Lessons**

SECTION 15 **Professional Development**

Schools are making encouraging progress in establishing citizenship as a secure part of the curriculum (see *Citizenship established? Citizenship in schools 2006/2009*, on the Ofsted website **www.ofsted.gov.uk/publications/090159**). This second edition of *100 Ideas for Teaching Citizenship* recognizes that huge achievement by teachers and the many others who help young people understand and become involved in democratic society.

This book provides up to date introductory material for teaching citizenship. There are also some challenging ideas for those who are now experienced citizenship teachers.

Citizenship and citizenship education are too controversial and contested, and young people learn in too many varied contexts, for anyone to be able to provide all the answers. Those involved in citizenship education should engage in a healthy and lively debate that is itself an indication of a democratic pluralistic society. There should never be one form of citizenship education. But there can be greater clarity about the key issues. Citizenship education must be coherent with explicitly understood opportunities for progression. I have tried to provide ideas, suggestions of resources and illustrations of activities that can be valued and enjoyed by learners. When factual information has been included my intention is to encourage teachers to promote the understanding, skills and dispositions associated with active citizenship.

When I have given ideas for citizenship education through other subjects (such as history) I want the focus to remain clearly on the essentials of citizenship. There should be an integrated approach to knowledge and skills so that young people can learn to think and act through their exploration of social and political issues in a modern multi-faith liberal democracy.

This book will be good for a positive, creative and democratic form of citizenship education if teachers and others are sufficiently stimulated, in a constructively critical manner, to try out some of the ideas and then develop their own.

Ian Davies

SECTION

1

Fundamental Contexts for Citizenship

IDEA

1

Citizenship

T. H. Marshall in *Citizenship and Social Class* suggested that during the 18th century, property rights had been recognized and so led to a form of civil citizenship; in the 19th century, as more people were allowed to vote, political rights grew; and in the 20th century, welfare developed, showing that social rights are important. Not everyone accepts Marshall's ideas, but much of the current educational policy emerges at least in part from his characterization of citizenship.

There are two competing citizenship traditions: the liberal (rights based) and the civic republican (based around notions of duties or responsibilities). Increasingly, there is reference made to a possible third tradition that relates to communitarianism. There are many other vitally important characterizations of citizenship that emphasize identity ('What sort of citizen are you?') as well as duties and rights.

Key questions include: is there too much freedom for young people today? Should I be forced to keep the law even if it is not just? Should I give to charitable causes? Some claim that rights and duties are ultimately hard to distinguish (is it my right or duty, as a parent, to look after my children?) but even so it may be worth using these labels as a way of helping young people to understand debates about today's societal issues.

Citizenship education develops young people who are intelligent, active and considerate. This focus on understanding and skills is very different from exclusively teaching academic knowledge, telling people how to follow rules or prioritizing personal issues (such as one's own diet or friendship groups).

KEY TEXT:

Heater, D. (1999), *What is Citizenship?* Cambridge, MA: Polity Press.

No one wants to waste time learning irrelevant information suitable only for a pub quiz. Old-fashioned civics courses have little to do with citizenship education. But if students are to be able to engage in debates and other activities they should have relevant knowledge. Depending on the educational purpose of the activity being studied, it's useful to know the basics of local government (the role of councillors and the extent of their decision-making power), national government (the system of elections, role of an MP, role of ministers), international organizations (G8, United Nations, European Union) and the key issues that dominate the UK and the world (currently terrorism, the environment, discrimination and prejudice and North–South relations).

Four key areas are:

1. political concepts (e.g. power, authority, justice);
2. political institutions (elected and nominated);
3. issues (either generally phrased, for example, terrorism; or, connected more directly to specific events or contexts, for example, the issue of Afghanistan);
4. political skills and dispositions appropriate for a democracy (making a case, discussion, debate about political issues).

One idea to try out: What qualities should a politician have? Diamond rank a series of qualities (skills/characteristics/attributes) and ask small groups of students to justify their decisions. Diamond ranking means ordering statements to show the perceived relative importance or significance with the first X the most important and the bottom X the least important, that is,

X
XX
XXX
XX
X

Statements could include: honesty; good public speaker; intelligent; healthy; hard working; looks good on TV; able to write so that many people understand; good organizer; strong personal beliefs.

Using a diamond rank allows students to debate and discuss. They shift the slips of paper into different positions easily as the discussion develops. This activity allows people to reach clear conclusions (which helps as each small group feeds back to the whole class) and emphasizes the process of active discussion that is necessary for decision making.

KEY TEXT (WITH LOTS OF ACTIVITIES FOR TEACHING):

Huddleston, T. (2004), *Citizens and Society: political literacy teacher resource pack*. London: Hodder and Stoughton.

The creation and distribution of wealth is obviously centrally relevant to citizenship because it tells us about issues of power, equality and justice. Many (often US) commentators point to what they see as a close connection between economic liberalism and political freedom. Others worry about the need to restrain the market for the sake of a decent society. These matters have been emphasized very strongly in light of the economic crisis that really began to catch the headlines with the difficulties at Northern Rock (http://news.bbc.co.uk/1/hi/in_depth/business/2008/northern_rock/default.stm) and took off into global frenzy with the collapse of Lehman Brothers (see http://business.timesonline.co.uk/tol/business/industry_sectors/banking_and_finance/article4761892.ece). These news stories can highlight the panic that we witnessed in 2008–2010 and so motivate students to learn.

There are three key questions that could be considered in order to develop a good citizenship education programme that relates to economics:

1. **Private or public?** A simple continuum of Market – Government could be written on one piece of paper with students placing the following at their preferred points (health; education; law and order; the army; coal industry; steel industry; ship building; railways; farming; fishing; forestry; housing);
2. **What can governments do?** The broad brush of what the government does could be explored by providing some background on the Treasury (see http://www.hm-treasury.gov.uk/). A government spending review provides an ideal opportunity to analyze decision-making. How much of the 'cake' would students like to see spent on defence, education, welfare, etc.? (More able students can think about the details of foreign exchange, taxation, money supply, inflation and unemployment).
3. **What should an individual do?** Exploring the nature of enterprise is a useful way to promote

understanding about the connection between individual responsibility and national and international issues (see www.young-enterprise.org.uk/)

The Economics and Business Studies Association is a good contact (see www.ebea.org.uk/home/); there are good resources at www.bized.co.uk/ and at www.pfeg.org.uk; and, many local authorities have a business education partnership team.

The law, and whether or not it is the same thing as justice, is a fundamental aspect of citizenship education. Learning about the law can be difficult but there is an excellent publication available which explains key features of the legal system and how it applies to young people (see www.citizenshipfoundation.org.uk/main/resource.php?s311).

There are very many examples of good activities that focus on the law.

1. 'ages and actions' – the teacher could draw up a list of activities – e.g. buying and drinking alcohol alone in a pub; getting married without parental permission; joining the army without parental permission – and ask students to speculate on the age at which these things may be done legally).
2. 'tough on crime, tough on the causes of crime' – students could debate what has helped, in July 2010, to achieve the lowest crime rates in 29 years – see www.bbc.co.uk/news/10645702 . They could debate 3 things: individual responsibility, the impact of context (economic climate, schools, family, etc.) and the role of punishments such as fines, Anti-Social Behaviour Orders (ASBO) and prisons (an interesting discussion about prisons is shown at www.esrcsocietytoday.ac.uk/ESRCInfoCentre/about/CI/CP/Our_Society_Today/Spotlights_2006/prison.aspx).

Many organizations exist to bring the law to life. Mock trials can be conducted and perhaps the best known service for mock trials in the UK is the Bar National Mock Trial competition (see www.citizenshipfoundation.org.uk/main/comps.php?21). An historical example of a mock trial, exploring the Amistad case, can be seen at: http://projects.edtech.sandi.net/hoover/amistad/. A visit to a magistrates' court can be a very valuable experience and I've found there's a definite commitment to education on the part of magistrates. A visit needs to be carefully handled: it can be voyeuristic; individuals known to the young people might be involved; the seating arrangements can make it difficult for all to hear what is going on; there can be a lot of administrative and technical material to deal with; and there will be unexpected developments such as last minute cancellations. Perhaps consider inviting a magistrate who is a good communicator to school. (For guidelines from another context on inviting speakers to school see www.ncb.org.uk/pdf/SEF_External_visitors_and_SRE_10.pdf).

Identity is, obviously, a vital part of citizenship. Identity and diversity (following the Ajegbo report – available on the Department for Education web pages) are now given explicit attention. We are citizens and we need to ask what that means for us as individuals and as members of groups. Much of this will be expressed through law, politics, economics and other fundamental matters.

There is certainly an overlap between citizenship identities and with what some might see as psychological matters (am I enterprising, extrovert, cautious or whatever) and cultural issues (does the group I see myself belonging to present itself as conservative, high status, religious, rebellious, etc.). There are many links between cultural and psychological issues. Gender is vitally important in relation to identity (psychologically, culturally and in other ways).

It is not acceptable to adopt a tokenistic approach in which we learn about a 'minority'. It is wrong to generalize inappropriately (e.g. some recent educational initiatives have been interpreted – if not always intended – as ways of combating the extremism of the 'other'). Generally, it is necessary to be clear in one's own mind about the relationship between the personal and the political. Perhaps in debates and other activities with students we need to reflect on three key questions:

1. Who am I (and is this determined by biology, by national/international society, by culture, by individual will);
2. What am I entitled to do and why;
3. What sort of responsibilities do I have to myself and to others.

These fundamental questions can then be developed by reference to contexts and case studies (two are shown below):

4. Do I expect the same of everyone or do I allow for variation depending on particular conditions

(e.g. religion, gender, perceived individual ability and circumstances);

5. Does it matter if I think one thing and do another (e.g. many people in public life have gotten into difficulties when advocating one thing for the mass of the population – such as state education – and then doing something else for their own family).

SECTION
2

Key Goals for Citizenship

IDEA

6

Justice

Michael Sandel has written an excellent book (see the key text below) which should be read by all citizenship teachers. He gives a large number of fascinating case studies that help us explore the idea and practice of justice. Many of his examples could be used directly in schools with only minor alterations for many classes:

1. What should the driver of a runaway train do if it is possible to avoid killing a group of people, only by going off the track and definitely killing a bystander?;
2. If soldiers who are injured in war time are automatically awarded a medal, should this include those who desert due to mental illness or those who have injured themselves through carelessness?;
3. What sort of justification would be needed to change the rules of a sport (if a disabled golfer wanted to use a golf cart, would that be acceptable or would that alter the game unfairly)?

Sandel's great contribution is to help us consider the ways in which we could resolve these issues. He suggests three possible ways: the greatest good for the greatest number (a sort of Benthamite utility); a justice is blind approach where you make a decision on broad principle without knowing how the outcome will impact you (this is the approach put forward by Rawls); the determination to say what is right in a particular context ('this may be the general principle but in this case it is right to . . .').

There are obvious disadvantages if every class were to focus on a series of dilemmas that led to unresolved disagreements between students. At the same time there are weaknesses in always and narrowly leading the students to the 'obvious' right answer. But if the debate is real and the *reasons* for coming to a decision (individually and/or collectively) are clear then there is the potential for some very valuable educational work.

KEY TEXT:

Sandel, M. J. (2009), *Justice: what's the right thing to do?* London: Allen Lane.

There are different sorts of rights and different ways in which they can be applied. For some, human rights is a much better basis for education than citizenship. Citizenship is, some argue, intrinsically exclusive. Governments can easily identify who is a citizen and who is not. This is an interesting position at a time when refugees, asylum seekers and immigration in general is a hot political topic. Does an emphasis on citizenship allow for people to be more easily removed from a place in which they are not entitled to the same rights as others? Human rights, however, may be similarly problematic. Some accuse the proponents of human rights as seeking only domination of the west; some suggest that human rights have no real force as national governments are, in reality, the decision makers; others feel that the idea of human rights has not been developed in a philosophically coherent manner.

A teacher could establish a list of rights (to education, to a name, to practise religion, to avoid imprisonment without trial and so on – a good list, obviously, is one that is taken from the Universal Declaration of Human Rights). The class could then be asked to divide these rights into groups: the right to . . . ; the right not to . . . ; different types of rights (political, economic, cultural and so on). Then the class would be asked to suggest the types of people who would be accorded those rights (everyone; children; men; women; the old; the young, etc.). By the end of this sequence of activities, students could be asked (perhaps using Sandel's framework) if it is fair to award those rights to the groups that have been identified, who would enforce it, how and what consequences that would have.

IDEA

8

Responsibilities

As discussed above, it is important to think carefully about the relationship between, and the meaning of, responsibilities and rights. It is useful to see them distinctly and it is important to recognize the overlaps between them. I feel that it is unhelpful to say that rights are contingent on responsibilities (if that were the case then the very old, the very young and those with disabilities who find it difficult, if not impossible, to fulfil certain obligations might be unfairly restricted in their rights).

It is useful to encourage young people to think about the limits of their responsibilities. A rather traditional exercise can help students think about the importance of keeping to the rules. A journey to school can take a very long time (if it takes place at all) and would be very dangerous if rules are not followed. Students can be asked to write a short story in which breakfast is never eaten or has not been subject to hygienic production, cars will not stop at traffic lights, teachers will not turn up on time, the vulnerable at school will experience serious challenges, etc. But then students could be asked to think about whether it is always necessary to follow what one is expected to do. In very immediate circumstances, should we always do what we are told?

Other broader case studies are possible:

When do we have a responsibility to go to war? When we are threatened; when we need to help people who are being treated badly; when supplies of natural resources on which we depend may be cut off; when not to act would probably encourage terrorists to increase their level of threat; when we need to put ourselves in a powerful position with an ally which is a stronger country. All of these – none of them?

A debate about our responsibilities in relation to Iraq in the 1990s and early 21st century would be very interesting and there is plenty of valuable source material easily available (see Tony Blair's *A Journey*).

In the UK we are very fortunate to enjoy the many benefits of a democratic society. Who could ever disagree with democracy (apart from a few crazed dictators)? That said, Bernard Crick (architect of citizenship education in England and many other countries) used to argue that politics (the creative reconciliation of different interest groups) had to take priority over democracy. It is not easy to advocate the sort of democracy that achieves just enough support (the US politician Karl Rove was not nicknamed Mr 51 per cent as a compliment, but rather in recognition of what some felt was his ability as a rather devious fixer). Local, European and other elections provide a wealth of fascinating data. Below I focus on some limited data from a few general elections.

Winning prime minister	Share of *total* electorate	Number of MPs (from a total of approximately 650)
Churchill (1951)	41%	321
Thatcher (1983)	32%	397
Blair (2005)	22%	356
Cameron (2010)	23.5%	307

Of course, the snapshot figures given above are not enough to gain a proper understanding of the situation. A good analysis of the 2010 result can be seen at http://news.bbc.co.uk/1/shared/election2010/results/ and the Political Studies Association site is a useful portal (see www.psa.ac.uk/)

Students could be asked:

1. Is it possible to identify a trend from the above turnout data?
2. Are you concerned about the data shown above?

What, if anything, should be done?

In relation to the last question, all sorts of options could be posed: should young people in school be very strongly encouraged to vote? (Or, perhaps told they must vote?) Should voting be compulsory for adults? (It is compulsory in some countries such as Australia). Should politicians be more reliable; honest; and, better communicators? Should electronic systems be used to make voting easier (e.g. one could vote from a mobile phone)? Should we introduce a new system of electing a government, e.g. Alternative Vote (AV) in which the voter has the chance to rank the candidates or another form of proportional representation – see www.politics.co.uk/briefings-guides/issue-briefs/legal-and-constitutional/proportional-representation-$366642.htm)?

IDEA

10

Diversity

The UK is, and always has been, a diverse society. The benefits of such a society are obvious and are to be celebrated. A vibrant, pluralistic society is a more prosperous, decent and interesting place to live than one in which there are constant invented divisions between 'us' and 'them'. In the UK (as in many other countries) we have experienced several phases in education and elsewhere of characterizing diversity. Prior to the 1960s, assimilation was expected in which 'guests' were supposed to adhere to the ways of the 'hosts'. This racist approach was replaced in the 1970s by a form of multiculturalism that came, negatively, to be referred to as the 3 Ss – saris, samosas and steel bands (in other words the 'other' was exotic, colourful, something of wonder, a display that emphasized difference and changed nothing). In the 1980s, a harder edged approached emerged in the form of anti-racism. This political drive was too much for some who felt it was confrontational. Currently, intercultural education is more common where there is an emphasis on culture (as well as politics) and an expectation that there will be interaction and exchange without the sense of 'guest' and 'host'.

'All different; all the same' is the slogan often used by the Council of Europe. Too much uniformity leads to assimilation; too much difference leads to unhelpful separation. Students could ask 'what is diversity?' Students write down the things that make us different and the things that make us the same. The lists usually appear very similar. We live in families – my family is not the same as yours; we have hair – mine is a different colour from yours; and so on. Another exercise is 'What can we do to stop racism?' Ask students to draw up a table with two columns: bad experiences; what could have been done to help. It will be easier to focus on everyday school experiences before moving onto bigger societal issues.

KEY TEXT:

Huddleston, T. (2007), *Identity, Diversity and Citizenship: a critical review of educational resources.* London: Association for Citizenship Teaching.

SECTION 3

Dimensions and Debates

IDEA

11

Gender

In 2008 the International Trade Union Confederation published a report on the 'global gender pay gap' in which they suggested 'Despite decades of anti-discrimination legislation and changes in company rhetoric, women, whether they are in New York or Shanghai, find their paycheck contains on average sixteen per cent less than male coworkers'. They claimed that even highly educated women were disadvantaged. Students could be asked to consider whether or not this is fair. In the UK there used to be an Equal Opportunities Commission which dealt with issues of gender. Since 2007 (following the Equality Act of 2006) a new body – the Equality and Human Rights Commission – works on issues to do with gender, disability and 'race'. The new organization makes it clear that interactions between areas relevant to inequality are important.

Ask students to consider the nature/nurture debate. At school are boys better (or worse) than some things than girls? Are boys better mathematicians; are girls better linguists? Is this due to the ways in which our brains work or have we been taught to be different? Generally, are boys more or less mature, noisier, more extroverted than girls or is that just a stereotype? When boys get jobs are they more suited to certain roles than girls (women in World War II were not allowed to fight as Spitfire pilots – was this fair?) Do women need special consideration (e.g. should a woman should be entitled to a longer period of maternity leave than the paternity leave available to men; should a woman be expected to receive preferential treatment from courts that are making decisions about child care following divorce.

Ask students to devise a school policy to avoid sexual discrimination. Focus on direct discrimination (e.g. girls not allowed to take part in certain activities; harassment is banned) and indirect discrimination (e.g. if an activity takes place at a certain time or is advertised in a certain way, it may appeal more to one sex than the other but it is theoretically open to everyone).

IDEA

12

Britishness

How would your students reply if someone asked them if they are English/Welsh/Scottish/British? Do the young people in your classes know what the difference is between Britain and the UK? What do they think about the positions of the main political parties on the question of Britain?

All politicians are keen to declare their patriotism. Gordon Brown, as a Scottish MP (and a prime minister of the UK until 2010), was very keen on promoting Britishness. David Cameron is an MP for an English constituency and Prime Minister of the UK, but the Conservative Party has little popularity in Scotland, Wales or Northern Ireland. Very different rules apply in different parts of the UK. There are, for example, big differences regarding university tuition fees, prescription charges, and so on. Many books are written about what it means to belong to a national group (e.g. Jeremy Paxman's 'The English'). Some suggest that there are national characteristics (and some suggest that this is an unacceptable generalization that leads to racism).

Some of the emphasis on the need for Britishness has come about as a reaction to the 2005 bombs in London which were planted by British citizens. Some responded by saying they were shocked that these murders could be committed against their own people; others were shocked because murder could be done at all. It is easy in these situations to become involved in highly sensitive debates – careful handling is essential.

Ask students: 'Is there something distinct about being British; or, should we focus on the experience of living in Britain?' Bernard Crick tended to favour the latter approach. The Life in the UK test' (see www.britishtest.com/ad) is an excellent way of exploring the knowledge and cultural awareness of students. Students can be asked what it means if they pass or fail the test. Do they think knowledge of these things is important or not? Do they think that people who are already citizens should not be required to know these things, but that other people who want to acquire citizenship should take the test? What attitude would they have if they wanted citizenship of another country? Would they willingly take the test for that country?

Some of the issues discussed above about Britishness are connected with immigration and migration. It is, of course, very important to understand the nature of diversity and citizenship. People of all nationalities live in Britain; members of very many ethnic groups are British citizens. It is useful to ensure that hard information is used as opposed to silly and potentially dangerous scare stories. Approximately 7.5 per cent of people in Britain were born abroad (http://news.bbc.co.uk/1/shared/spl/hi/uk/05/born_abroad/html/overview.stm). The 2001 census showed that 86 per cent of people in the UK were 'white British' and a further 6 per cent 'white other'. Information about passports and immigration may be seen through various government offices (especially the Home Office – www.homeoffice.gov.uk/passports-and-immigration/). The UK population in 2010 is approximately 61.8 million. This is, approximately, an increase of 5 per cent since 1999, but any change is due to many factors (birth rate, deaths as well as migration). Population decline has occurred in 38 local authorities. The Office for National Statistics (www.statistics.gov.uk/statbase/product.asp?vlnk=15106) gives the detail behind these headline figures.

Ask students to investigate the following statement:

In September 2010 Vince Cable (Business Secretary) spoke about restrictions on immigration: 'The brutal fact is that the way the system is currently being applied is very damaging. We have now lots of case studies of companies which are either not investing or relocating or in many cases just not able to function effectively because they cannot get key staff – management, specialist engineers and so on – from outside the European Union'.

Students should ask: how many people have moved in and out of the UK during the last ten years?; Where have they come from and gone to?; How much movement takes place within the EU, where fewer restrictions apply about the movement of people, as compared with movement to and from other countries?; What types of people (men/women/young/old/skilled/unskilled etc.)

have moved?; Why do people move (for jobs, to escape persecution, to be with family members, to live a better life)?; Should there be limits to the numbers of people moving out of a country?; Should there be limits to the numbers of people moving into a country?; If there are to be limits then how can they be decided?

Barack Obama was elected as President of the United States in 2008 following a campaign in which there was a great deal of sophisticated use of 'new' technology (use of web sites, blogging, social network sites). In the various countries of Eastern Europe, Egypt and elsewhere, activists are turning to e-democracy. They claim that the technology is available to everyone, easy to use, fast and exciting. They say that it is not just a means of doing the same things better, but because it is not restricted in the same way as older media, it is intrinsically more democratic. Now, of course, there are arguments against this position: new technology is actually still available only to the minority who live in relatively rich countries; it can be used as much by established authorities as by activist groups; most of its uses by young people is for social purposes; in schools it is often simply used for better presentations rather than collaborative learning; and, it encourages the use of sound bites rather than helping in the development of careful, intelligent critical reflection about serious issues. Perhaps one of the most surprising things about the 2010 general election in the UK was the importance of the very traditional medium of television (principally in the form of formal debates between leading politicians) and the absence of new technology.

Ask students to do 4 things:

1. Create a poster using new technology and compare it with what could have been achieved using traditional art work;
2. Ask if they would be more likely to vote if they were able to do so using new technology rather than pen and paper in a polling booth;
3. Simultaneously send an email and a surface letter to a public figure and see how quickly and what sort of answers are given;
4. Set up a blog involving at least 5 people within the class on the theme of a current controversial issue.

Ask the participants whether they enjoyed the experience and what, if anything, they learned from it.

KEY TEXT:

Livingstone, S. (2009), *Children and the internet.* Cambridge, MA: Polity.

For some people, the city of God and the city of people are entirely different. Bernard Crick was a prominent figure in the humanist society. Richard Dawkins has written about the 'God Delusion'. The Pope, during his visit to the UK in 2010, referred to 'extreme secularism'.

It is difficult to be precise about the size of faith groups. The 2001 census showed that 72 per cent were Christian and 3 per cent Muslim (but then the reliability of the figures may be thrown into doubt when in 2007 the Tearfund Survey came up with the very different figure that 53 per cent of people declared themselves to be Christian; and, in the 2001 census 390,000 people declared themselves, when referring to religion, to be Jedi knights).

And yet, faith is a very serious issue indeed in relation to citizenship. During and after his time as Prime Minister, Tony Blair emphasized the significance of faith schools. This opportunity has continued with David Cameron's 'big society' and the chance to establish 'free schools'. The increased construction of buildings for several faith groups in all major UK cities is very noticeable. Key individuals who are active in the field of citizenship education are affiliated to religious groups. Paul J. Weithman has argued that religion and the obligations of citizenship are not in tension. He suggests that religion helps develop a decent community and offers a voice for the marginalized.

Analyze the case of children (aged 4–11) who went to the Roman Catholic Holy Cross school in Northern Ireland which is located in a Protestant area. The children were threatened. Riot police were present. Some details about the case may be seen at www.guardian.co.uk/world/2001/sep/04/qanda.schools Students could be asked to come up with a solution that places the school in the context of the Northern Ireland peace process and suggests possibilities for action by individual teachers and families.

KEY TEXT:

Arthur, J., Gearon, L., Sears, A. (2010), *Education, Politics and Religion: Reconciling the Civic and the Sacred in Education*. London: Routledge.

SECTION

4

UK and International Governmental Bodies

IDEA

16

House of Parliament/Number 10 Downing Street

The Number 10 website (www.number10.gov.uk/) helps students learn a little about the Prime Minister and his office. The virtual tour of the house is interesting as a bit of tourism and may help students feel that real people live and work in the house. The site is attractive, user friendly, up to date and with the latest political announcements often on video. A class could review a set of newspapers for one day, to choose an issue that seems important to them and then ask a question or express their views to the PM. (Unfortunately, responses are no longer guaranteed to email, so surface mail would need to be used.)

There is a parliamentary education unit which produces resources for school students and teachers (see www.parliament.uk/directories/educationunit.cfm). It can be important for young people to know how a bill becomes law, what an MP does and what the difference is between the front and back benches. But I suggest that it is often more useful and more interesting to think about individuals (perhaps a case study on a local MP or follow the 'MP for a week' game), issues (should we have nuclear weapons?) and what key concepts can be raised (who really has power within the House of Commons – are the debates necessary and effective?). Many teachers have established mock parliamentary debates with roles for different political parties and then revealed what actually happened by showing pages from the Hansard record.

A visit to the Houses of Parliament (perhaps this is possible only for London based schools?) can be valuable, especially if arrangements can be made to be met by one's MP and for the students to see something happening in the chamber. If one were to make such a visit, it would be good to include another group of people who are involved in the democratic process (perhaps a pressure group?) in another part of the day.

IDEA 17

The Treasury

HM Treasury is responsible for formulating and putting into effect the UK Government's financial and economy policy; the 2010 budget statement focused on the key targets of deficit reduction, enterprise and fairness (www.hm-treasury.gov.uk/). The Treasury is concerned with promoting awareness of its work (although the site has recently become much more serious and students should be prepared very thoroughly in advance if they are to use it effectively).

One way of helping students to understand a little about economic decision making would be to explain the reasons for taxation: i.e., revenue (money is raised for schools, roads, defence, etc.); redistribution (the poor are helped and the industrious are rewarded); repricing (people are discouraged from having 'bad' things like alcohol by increasing the price); representation (it is commonly believed that all those who pay tax have a say in the government but, of course, this is not quite true as indirect taxation is paid by many, including children, who do not have a vote).

Guidance on tax allowances (www.hmrc.gov.uk/rates/it.htm) and national insurance (www.hmrc.gov.uk/ni/intro/basics.htm#4) may help those students who can cope with detail. For most students it might work best to develop an exercise in which they are allocated a notional £100 and remove £20 for tax (a certain amount of invention is taking place here and I am not including national insurance which is charged at approximately 10 per cent over a certain wage and not asking them to consider indirect taxation such as value added tax (VAT) which is currently 20 per cent). Provide the class with a list of salaries (starting at £10k and going up in bands of £5k up to £40k) and with a list of products (newspapers, bread, alcohol, clothes, children's toys, etc.). Now ask students to decide on levels of direct and indirect taxation. They should justify their answers using the categories above (revenue; redistribution; repricing and representation) and then be asked to reflect on the real rates. For the more able, discussions can take place about the connection between political ideas and taxation (very generally, the right wing position is to be in favour of lowering direct taxation).

The Home Office (www.homeoffice.gov.uk/) is the lead government department for immigration and passports, drugs policy, crime, counterterrorism and police.

The Home Office may be one of the key organizations that can be seen as attempting to promote citizenship as well as offering opportunities for the study of citizenship. In its concerns with asylum seekers a key feature of citizenship (formal legal status) can be examined. It would be useful to examine specific cases of individuals who have not been granted asylum status (ask whether the students think that justice was achieved).

Crime is obviously a centrally relevant issue to citizenship. There are cases of people taking individual action. Bernard Goetz in New York (see http://en.wikipedia.org/wiki/Bernhard_Goetz) shot four young men who were threatening him. His sentence for illegal possession of a firearm was controversial.

In the UK there are frequent media reports and discussions which focus on the question of when one is allowed to take action against those whom we feel intend to hurt us. The general common law principle was stated in *Beckford v. R,* (1988) 1 AC 130: 'A defendant is entitled to use reasonable force to protect himself, others for whom he is responsible and his property. It must be reasonable'. What do students think is meant by 'reasonable force'?

The Olympics of 2012 promises to be a wonderful occasion but it will also be extremely difficult for police. Students could be asked to read the Home Office details at www.homeoffice.gov.uk/counter-terrorism/securing-2012-olympic-games/ and then to consider an invented list of things that they as spectators would tolerate. Closed-circuit television (CCTV) in all venues and in all public places; every spectator to be searched; every applicant for a ticket to be the subject of police enquiries (this would probably not involve face-to-face interviews but would involve scrutiny of bank accounts); very heavy police presence (the ratio of 1 police officer to 20 spectators). If all these things are acceptable, what would be unacceptable and why?

IDEA

19

The Foreign Office

The Foreign and Commonwealth Office (www.fco.gov.uk/en/) is responsible for promoting British interests abroad. There is a global network of offices (embassies, High Commissions and consulates in 170 countries).

An endless range of teaching issues arise from the work of the Foreign Office. A number of countries are regarded as difficult. It would be interesting to set up a project around North Korea. Where is it? Who is the political leader? What have western leaders said about North Korea? Is it really a threat to peace and security? And then more particularly, would it be right for a government minister to visit the country? If so, what are the options that are open to the minister and what should he do and not do? Links could be made in these discussions with ideas of global citizenship.

The choice of country to investigate can be more or less controversial. North Korea is, in some ways, less controversial to study at the moment than Iran (about which some prominent public figures, such as Tony Blair, are making rather firm and negative statements). Iraq and Afghanistan are perhaps most controversial of all. This does not mean that students should not be asked to learn about these countries, but a great deal of sensitivity and professional skill will be required (many students will know people who have direct experience with these countries).

An interesting case study could be done around Robin Cook's statement about an 'ethical foreign policy' which he came to regret. Is it possible to work ethically in foreign affairs? Discussions about the extent to which UK politicians knew about the illegal activities of intelligence organizations, which may have involved torture, are important (even if they are difficult to teach about).

There are many excellent resources available. One that might be very useful (although it is challenging in a number of ways and was published some time ago) is Pike, G. and Selby, D. (1988), *Global Teacher, Global Learner*. London: Hodder and Stoughton.

Students could explore international and global themes by investigating the work of the Department for International Development (DFID) (www.dfid.gov.uk). There is a wealth of educational resources for exploring the global dimension (e.g. see www.globaldimension.org.uk/) and it is worth exploring associations and networks (e.g. the Development Education Association).

Two fascinating ideas which I have adapted from the global dimension site are:

1. Students are presented with a series of pictures which may say something about the interlocking nature of the world. A variegated leaf; an estuary with many small tributaries; a stained glass window made up of many small parts to make one picture. They will probably get the point immediately and make comments about overlap and interaction. The small parts of the world being combined to make one coherent and beautiful whole. But then show another set of pictures: a pile of individual pieces of mixed fruit (oranges, apples, bananas), a border crossing, a bank of fog. Are these more accurate symbols of what the world is like: barriers, separate elements and an inability to see what is needed? When we cooperate with others, do we preserve our separate identity or do we really interconnect? This is a good way to talk about the distinction between international work (literally, between the nations) and global partnerships in which there is full integration. Finally, show a series of pictures of bridges and ask what sort of links we want to make and with whom;
2. A series of (carefully chosen) photos can be shown of the floods in Pakistan and another part of the world in which there are extreme weather conditions (e.g. New York in the winter; certain cities in the Middle East which experience very high temperatures; Tokyo which is frequently hit by earthquakes and typhoons). Questions may be asked about what is meant by a 'natural' disaster. If some people suffer more than

others, then what is really causing hardship? If the photos show people, questions may be developed about what they are thinking and what they can do to help themselves and their families.

IDEA

21

The Department for Education

The National Curriculum is always the subject of fierce debate. Opinions vary as to whether Citizenship Education is a specialist subject or something that all teachers are involved with in their daily professional duties. I think that teaching people about contemporary society and how they can contribute to it is important and needs to be tackled explicitly and professionally by teachers who have more than a passing interest in it. If a history teacher was asked to teach science we would raise an eyebrow. Unless we feel that the controversial issues in contemporary society are just plain common sense then we need some proper professional focus.

It is worth reviewing the latest position of the Department for Education. The current web site does not show much that is explicitly about citizenship education but guidance will be forthcoming. There will also be material from other government departments and agencies (e.g. the Training and Development Agency for Schools). Previously produced resources are still of great value. The 'school self-evaluation tool' was produced in 2004. Building on research being undertaken by the National Foundation for Educational Research and others it suggests that schools are at different stages of development in relation to citizenship education. Some are at an early stage ('focusing') while others are either 'developing', 'established' or 'advanced'. Descriptions of these different levels are given in relation to leadership, resources and their management, teaching and learning, staff development, monitoring and evaluation, and parental/community involvement. The tool can be used by schools to reflect on where they might see themselves and how they might develop even further. Teachers will not want to accept all the advice but with a positive, critical perspective this tool will prove to be a useful addition to the school's armoury.

KEY TEXT:

Huddleston, T. and Kerr, D. (eds) (2006), *Making Sense of Citizenship: a continuing professional development handbook*. London: Citizenship Foundation/DfES.

IDEA

22

Ofsted

The office for standards in education has not always been entirely free from controversy. Hailed by some as the body responsible for preserving and developing high standards, it attracts fierce criticism from others. It cannot be ignored and its web site contains reports on each school in England and Wales as well as local authorities and providers of teacher education. The handbook of guidance for inspections is a vital resource (see www.ofsted.gov.uk/Ofsted-home/Forms-and-guidance). The key is to gain precise understanding about what the inspectors value. This does not mean a slavish adherence to government targets but it does mean that there should be clear and specific understanding about what is deemed as 'good work'. Teachers should consider, by reviewing academic results and less tangible indications of the quality of learning and personal development, not only how well they are managing to achieve in relation to their own targets (generally and for individuals) but also how this compares across subjects and other schools.

Reports on citizenship education by Ofsted have become increasingly positive. The most recent report (*Citizenship established? Citizenship in schools 2006/9)* 'shows schools are making encouraging progress in establishing citizenship as a secure part of the curriculum, with just over half of the secondary schools visited judged good or outstanding for students' achievement in their knowledge and learning'. The inspectors found the highest standards in schools where there were dedicated and regular spaces on the timetable. Sharing a timetable spot with Personal, Social and Health Education (PSHE) was felt to be confusing. Those schools that placed too much emphasis on special collapsed timetable days did not achieve as much as others. There is also an indication that some schools are still not providing a coherent programme but instead concentrating on specific issues that are of interest to the teachers. Leadership for citizenship is seen as essential. These findings seem persuasive as they are in agreement with the conclusions drawn by researchers.

The standards for teaching should be essential reading for all teachers. The standards provide an indication of what is officially regarded as necessary work for beginning teachers and outline what needs to be done by more experienced teachers.

The TDA funded citizED (www.citized.info) which, as well as organizing conferences and running research and development projects, produced resources in four areas (primary; secondary; post 16 and cross-curricular).

There are now specialist programmes in initial teacher education in citizenship and a programme of continuing professional development which is managed by the Association for Citizenship Teaching in collaboration with a range of bodies including the Citizenship Foundation.

Some of the key priorities for trainee teachers are:

1. Producing a subject audit. How does their degree compare with the demands of the National Curriculum, other examination syllabuses and topics of contemporary significance?
2. Learning how to focus a lesson so that key learning outcomes are identified and achieved. Trainee teachers have to be helped to understand that getting students to argue with each other is not enough.
3. Writing practical exercises. Trainee teachers often need help to move between the stages of a lesson. Most lessons will contain a phase in which explanations are given; there then comes a crucial phase in which instructions are given. Often at the point at which students need to be told what to do, the trainees feel that they have already done their job and that students will somehow be able to get on with things. This point is the time at which success can be achieved or disaster will occur. Trainees need to be told explicitly what to do.
4. Developing assessment. Trainees will need to understand the details given in the National Curriculum and they will need to know how to use a

range of data (oral, written) gathered over a period of time. They will need to think about how these assessments will help shape their future teaching. They will need to think how to report to others about the progress being made by students.

KEY TEXT:

Gearon, L. (ed.) (2010), *Learning to teach citizenship in the secondary school*. Abingdon, UK: Routledge.

The government web pages for the Ministry of Justice include the following statement:

'The Ministry of Justice works to protect the public and reduce re-offending, and to provide a more effective, transparent and responsive criminal justice system for victims and the public. We also provide fair and simple routes to civil and family justice. The Ministry of Justice has responsibility for different parts of the justice system – the courts, prisons, probation services and attendance centres'.

The responsibilities of this Ministry are clearly related to citizenship. It would be educationally beneficial for students to investigate what is done and in what ways. There are opportunities for students to do more, however, than simply comprehend the work of the Ministry. It will be very stimulating for students to consider a range of cases which led to sentencing. This will give them an insight into the causes of crime, the types of people who commit crimes, the agencies involved in bringing people to justice (and the extent of their responsibilities), the use of evidence and the ways in which decisions are made in order to sentence a criminal.

At the time of writing the Ministry is offering a series of radio programmes in cooperation with the BBC about sentencing. The public is invited to engage with this process in ways that I feel will be very valuable. It can, however, be difficult to gain access to this sort of material at all times. How can students gain access to material about sentencing? I hesitate to recommend something like the Judge Judy programmes. Often those programmes are negatively argumentative, based around personality rather than principles of justice and too brief to allow for proper reflection. But with careful handling and with teachers prepared to help students see the inadequacies of the TV presentation, perhaps some good work could be done. (In a similar way popular phone-in programmes can be seen as citizenship lessons which need to be professionally shaped if citizenship education is to occur).

IDEA

25

The United Nations

A clear overview of the United Nations can be seen at: www.un.org/en/aboutun/index.shtml

The UN was set up in 1945 with 50 countries working 'to maintain international peace and security; to develop friendly relations among nations; to cooperate in solving international economic, social, cultural and humanitarian problems and in promoting respect for human rights and fundamental freedoms; and to be a centre for harmonizing the actions of nations in attaining these ends'. Key structures include the General Assembly, the International Court of Justice and the Security Council. The UN is not a world government and relies on support from members, especially those who belong to the Security Council. There is a United Nations Association for the UK (see www.una-uk.org/). One of the most common ways used by teachers to explore issues about the United Nations is to establish or become involved in a Model United Nations activity. If international visits are possible then this can be done in person (see www.worldmun.org/index.php) and there are also good teaching guides available for work in one's own school (see www.una.org.uk/education/index.html).

Students could be asked to learn more about the Millennium Development Goals and to track progress towards their achievement. The goals may be seen at: www.un.org/millenniumgoals/

It is useful to link work on the United Nations with other international organizations such as the World Trade Organization, the G8, etc. Reviews of the web pages provided by these organizations together with classroom activities can be very valuable. For example, illustrations can be given of disputes about subsidies. Start a lesson by sharing some sweets, asking about the price and suggesting that each person would in the near future have to pay three times as much in order to help the sugar producers in low-income countries. Some research would be needed using data from relevant web sites shown above as well as current media reports.

Students could present three points for and against the removal of subsidies from countries that are from the richer north of the world.

IDEA 26

The World Trade Organization

Law, economics and politics are given concrete expression in real world contexts. There are many institutions that are charged with responsibility for action in relation to citizenship and the World Trade Organization (WTO) is recognized as being influential. It was established in 1995 and is based in Geneva, Switzerland. It makes rules about international trade aiming to increase incomes and promote peace through trade. At a time of economic recession the need to ensure that trade grows and is managed in a fair manner is essential. There are 153 member-countries (in September 2010), who discuss and agree on such things as tariffs. The WTO has a number of functions:

1. administering WTO trade agreements
2. forum for trade negotiations
3. handling trade disputes
4. monitoring national trade policies
5. technical assistance and training for developing countries
6. cooperation with other international organizations.

Detailed reporting on the activities of the World Trade Organization can be seen at www.wto.org. It is possible to help students explore ways to develop trade fairly. The Doha Development Agenda is significant. Do students think that poor countries should be helped to trade with rich countries and, if so, how? Should special agreements be made to purchase products from low-income countries? These agreements might protect local farmers and guarantee, for example, that in the UK bananas are purchased from specific countries at an inflated price. This will help develop the economy of the low-income country, help save lives and ultimately, in the long term, ensure that rich countries have more markets to sell their goods. But what about the opposing arguments: is it acceptable that some people (but not the full population) in one country are given advantages; are other countries still neglected; is the environment damaged through excessive transport of goods as at least some of the products could be grown closer to the UK; are we forcing prices to be higher than they need to be?

IDEA

27

Agenda 21

Agenda 21 is not an organization but it is an extremely important international initiative. In 1992 the United Nations (UN) held an Earth Summit in Rio de Janeiro, Brazil. One outcome of this was the adoption of Agenda 21 by 178 governments. In 1999, the UK government produced its own plan for how it would help achieve the goals of Agenda 21. Many local authorities publicize their own work on their web sites, the Geographical Association and the Royal Geographical Society produce their own material and individual schools have reported on what they have done. Often these reports are given as part of 'Local Agenda 21' which, as the name suggests, is the attempt to make things happen in one's own area (e.g. www.la21.org.uk).

I have been involved in events that can be held in which school students from different local authorities came together to present the results of their research on climate change, recycling and waste management and to pose questions to an invited panel of politicians and environmentalists. Less ambitious work could take place by one class group investigating the transport preferences and practices of teachers and students when travelling to and from school. Ask students to develop and then present proposals to improve transport and ask those reading or listening to those proposals to evaluate them on the basis of criteria such as cost, likely popularity and positive impact on the environment. Alternatively, exploration could take place into a local controversial issue (e.g. are increased parking charges really 'green' or just another way of raising money?) The students could ask why it was done, what is the nature of the reactions, who is objecting, who is supportive, what alternatives are there and what might happen in the future. This could be achieved through several channels by

1. inviting different speakers into the classroom
2. reviewing newspapers reports
3. interviewing residents (or class members) about their views.

The G8 is described at: http://news.bbc.co.uk/1/hi/world/americas/country_profiles/3777557.stm Since 1975, the heads of state or government of the major industrial democracies have been meeting annually to deal with the major economic and political issues facing their domestic societies and the international community as a whole. The current members are France, the United States, Britain, Germany, Japan, Italy, Canada, the European and Russia. Summits deal with macroeconomic management, international trade and relations with developing countries as well as many other matters including energy, terrorism, crime, etc. In addition to the main summit there are supporting ministerial meetings. The summit sets priorities, defines new issues and provides guidance to established international organizations. The annual meeting has been an opportunity for antiglobalization demonstrations since the Birmingham Summit in 1998; the protests turned violent in 2001 at the Genoa Summit, resulting in the death of a protestor. For older and more academically able students there are opportunities to consider the extent to which countries actually meet their commitments given at previous meetings. Students could be asked to develop a list of reasons (going beyond a simple identification of greed) that might explain why the promises made by politicians are not always kept. Ask students to talk about this in pairs and then to share their reasoning in small groups. This could then lead to full class discussions.

For less able students there are many opportunities to review media reports about current or previous G8 summits. Some fairly simple questions could be posed about what the summit did but perhaps also a more focussed question could explore the actions of the protesters and the responses from the politicians. The summits are being held in increasingly isolated locations. Do students think that there is a need for this (for the safety of those who might protest and to ensure a secure environment where discussions by experts can occur) or do they feel that decisions should be made from public spaces? A focussed question could be: 'does the class think that it is acceptable for G8 summit to be held in an isolated location that is heavily guarded?'

30 per cent of the world's population in 54 independent states cooperate in the Commonwealth. The countries share a history (broadly, the organization has evolved from what was the British Empire). It aims to promote peace, democracy, equality and good governance with heads of government meeting every 2 years. Overviews of the work of the Commonwealth can be seen at www.thecommonwealth.org/ and there is a free publication ('Common Ground') that explains the structure, processes and issues (and there is also a resource called 'Young Commonwealth' which may be helpful in primary and lower secondary).

There is a good resource on the Teacher Training Resource Bank (ttrb) site (see www.ttrb.ac.uk) by Penelope Hartnett about how to use the British Empire and Commonwealth Museum in Bristol. For schools in that part of the country it is possible to have an enjoyable and rewarding experience during a visit. The second Monday in March is Commonwealth Day and this can be marked in various ways. Students can research individual countries with displays which carry information and/or there could be a more precise focus on issues (e.g. about poverty, HIV/AIDs, education, trade and so on). Cooperation with members of the Geography Department could be very useful. It will be important to ensure that citizenship issues remain at the forefront. Commonwealth Day can also provide an opportunity to develop discussions about ways to develop the Commonwealth as a whole. Should it be more democratic and if so how? Should the head of the Commonwealth always be the reigning British monarch? Should the official language always be English? Are sporting occasions valuable for the Commonwealth? How successful were the 2010 Commonwealth Games in India – how could they have been improved? The Royal Commonwealth Society (see www.thercs.org/youth) has a range of projects and resources. It is also worth exploring the opportunities offered by the

Commonwealth Education Trust (see www.cet1886.org). It is possible to set up a mock CHOGM (Commonwealth Heads of Government Meeting).

Full information about the European Union (27 countries) can be seen at: http://Europa.eu/index_en.htm There are several key EU institutions, each playing a specific role:

1. European Parliament (elected by the peoples of the Member States);
2. European Council (Sets the general political direction and priorities of the European Union);
3. European Commission (Appointed Commissioners and the EU's civil service. The Commission proposes EU legislation and checks it is properly applied across the EU. Works in the interests of the EU as a whole.);
4. Court of Justice (ensuring compliance with the law);
5. Court of Auditors (Reviews the financing of the EU's activities).

These are flanked by other important bodies including the European Economic and Social Committee (represents civil society, employers and employees); and the European Central Bank (responsible for monetary policy and managing the euro). The Council of Europe is also significant in cultural and educational matters.

An interesting class debate could involve discussing benefits/weaknesses of enlarging the EU: 'should Libya join the EU'?

1. Geography: Libya is part of Africa not Europe (but it is closer to some European capitals than parts of the UK; Russia is a member of the Council of Europe).
2. Culture: Christianity is a strong influence in the heritage of Europe but is it acceptable to exclude a state on the basis of its religion and, obviously, there are increasing numbers of people who are not Christians who are European).
3. Politics: Libya does not have a good record on human rights but the situation is improving (and the UK is one of those countries that has lost a case at the European Court of Human Rights).

Schools can take part in active projects (e.g. Comenius). Less ambitiously, a debate could take place whether the UK should join the euro involving the 'Euro party'; the 'Wait and See party' and 'Euro? Never!'. Each party should make a two minute statement followed by discussion around economics, democracy and identity. Interesting work can take place on European elections (turnout has steadily declined from 62 per cent in 1979 to 43 per cent in 2009 – see http://news.bbc.co.uk/1/hi/8088309.stm)

'The Council of Europe, based in Strasbourg (France), now covers virtually the entire European continent, with its 47 member countries. Founded on 5 May 1949 by 10 countries, the Council of Europe seeks to develop throughout Europe common and democratic principles based on the European Convention on Human Rights and other reference texts on the protection of individuals'.

The Council of Europe can appear bureaucratically daunting. In May 2010 for example Recommendation CM/Rec(2010)7 was adopted on Education for Democratic Citizenship and Human Rights Education. It is unlikely that many teachers will have this firmly in their minds as they plan their lessons and mark their books. And yet, the work of the Council of Europe is extremely important. These recommendations and other policy statements ensure that there is a platform for professionals to take action. A head teacher who needs to be convinced by the need for citizenship education might be impressed by the fact that 47 countries – including the UK – have just reaffirmed their commitment to it. The Council also offers many opportunities for teachers to join groups in which people from different countries compare resources and teaching approaches and plan how to do new things. The resources produced by the Council often provide an insight into how good practice may be further developed.

It is well worth the effort to look at the following resources: (www.coe.int/t/dg4/education/edc/3_RESOURCES/EDC_pack_en.asp)

1. key issues for EDC/HRE Policies
2. democratic Governance of Schools
3. How all teachers can support citizenship and human rights education: a framework for the development of competences?
4. Quality Assurance of Education for Democratic Citizenship in Schools
5. School-Community-University Partnerships for a Sustainable Democracy: Education for Democratic Citizenship in Europe and the United States

SECTION 5

Education Organizations/ NGOs

IDEA

32

The Citizenship Foundation

'We encourage and enable individuals to engage effectively in their communities and in democratic society at large'.

63 Gee Street, London EC1V 3RS
Tel: +44 (0)20 7566 4141
Email: info@citizenshipfoundation.org.uk
Web page: www.citizenshipfoundation.org.uk

The Citizenship Foundation (CF) focuses on better citizenship education ('We provide teachers and schools with the tools to deliver engaging and critical citizenship education'), effective participation ('We help people get to grips with civic engagement by working in their communities on issues that are important to them') and stronger communities ('We support voluntary, community and faith groups in pursuit of a more just, inclusive and cohesive society').

It began life as the Law in Education project and so it is not surprising that legal matters are still obviously represented in the work of the charity. It has, in recent years, been highly influential in the development of citizenship education and expanded its focus (and the number of its employees) to work on a wide range of matters (including community issues). CF has worked alone and with many other individuals and organizations to provide seminars for teachers, mock trial competitions, a wide range of educational resources (including a young person's passport which explains very many issues and is now in its 14th edition), lawyers in schools, charitable work, citizen manifestos and many other events and publications. Practical classroom resources are produced that are very valuable. Ted Huddleston, Don Rowe and Tony Thorpe are some of the people associated with the Foundation who write good classroom resources (e.g. see Tony Thorpe (2001), *Understanding Citizenship*. London: Hodder and Stoughton and the Citizenship Foundation).

'ACT is the professional subject association for those involved in citizenship education'.

63 Gee Street, London EC1V 3RS
Tel: 020 7367 0510
Email: info@teachingcitizenship.org.uk
Web page: www.teachingcitizenship.org.uk

ACT is an umbrella organization which emerged from close collaboration between a number of existing groups involved in citizenship education (such as the Citizenship Foundation and the Institute for Citizenship). It came into being as citizenship education was introduced into the National Curriculum to support teachers. It provides:

1. a magazine (Teaching Citizenship)
2. an annual conference
3. a twice-termly electronic newsletter
4. interesting lesson plans
5. links to useful resources such as training courses; assessment for citizenship and conferences

Its founding president was Professor Sir Bernard Crick and its current President is Jan Newton who previously led the Citizenship Foundation and the government's citizenship education team. Its chair is David Barrs (a head teacher) and its very active professional officer is Chris Waller. One of its great strengths is that it is a membership organization which not only provides a focus for key organizations but also allows individual teachers and others to become part of a group, strengthening their identity and confidence as they work for the further development of citizenship education.

IDEA

34

The Association for Teaching of Social Sciences (ATSS)

The ATSS, a registered charity, is a volunteer group of teachers who have joined together to further the interests of Social Science teaching in secondary schools, colleges and teacher training courses in higher education.

C/o The British Sociological Association
Palatine House, Belmont Business Park
Durham
Co. Durham
DH1 1TW
Tel: 0191 383 0839 Email: atss@btconnect.com
Web page: www.atss.org.uk/

Composed mainly of Sociologists, the ATSS also includes teachers of Psychology, Politics and Economics amongst its members. The Association also has close links with similar organizations such as the British Sociological Association, the Association for Psychology Teachers and the Economics and Business Education Association.

The aim of the Association is to encourage and promote the teaching of the Social Sciences in Primary, Secondary, Further and Higher Education. The Association therefore provides opportunities for those teaching in the Social Sciences to develop and share ideas and strategies for the promotion and delivery of the teaching of the Social Sciences. One of the main activities of the ATSS is the dissemination of information relating to teaching materials and teaching methods. The Association is also active in promoting the interests of Social Science teachers to examination boards, academic bodies, governmental and political agencies and the wider public.

Members receive:

1. three copies per year of the journal 'Social Science Teacher'.
2. an annual national conference for teachers and lecturers in the social sciences.
3. a regular newsletter.
4. a range of regional staff and student conferences.
5. a regularly updated website at www.atss.org.uk

237 Pentonville Road, London N1 9NJ, UK
Tel: 020 7278 6601
Web page: www.csv.org.uk/

Founded in 1962, Community Service Volunteers (CSV) is the UK's leading volunteering and training charity.CSV's vision is of a society where everyone can participate to build healthy, enterprising and inclusive communities.

Every year, CSV involves over 150,000 volunteers in high quality opportunities that enrich lives and tackle real need. Between them, they help transform the lives of more than 1 million people across the UK.

CSV trains more than 12,000 young people and adults each year, helping them build the skills and confidence they need to progress to further education or employment or to set up in business.

There are very many opportunities for people of all ages, dispositions and interests to become involved in community life in the UK and beyond. CSV has contributed hugely to the development of citizenship education and has led many projects and produced excellent educational resources. Courses are offered on conflict resolution, peer mentoring, leadership, etc.

IDEA

36

The Development Education Association

'DEA is an education charity that promotes global learning. We work to ensure that people in the UK learn about global issues such as poverty and climate change and develop an open-minded, global outlook. Our present focus is on schools and youth work. We work to change what people learn and how they learn, through influencing policy and improving educators' practice. Our national network of member organisations and supporters share our conviction that the role of education today is crucial in shaping a better tomorrow'.

CAN Mezzanine, 32–36 Loman Street, London SE1 0EH

Tel: 020 7922 7930

Email: dea@dea.org.uk/Web page: www.dea.org.uk

An important perspective on citizenship is provided by the DEA including, and taking us beyond, issues to do with legal status in national contexts and exploring matters from various countries to promote skills and dispositions. Various practical ways forward are possible. There is staff in Development Education Centres (DECs) in various parts of the country working with local secondary teachers on how to introduce global citizenship into their schools. There are many resources for schools including a global dimension web site and case studies of successful initiatives. Training is available for teachers. DEA is also very active in youth work.

'The Hansard Society is the UK's leading independent, non-partisan; political research and education charity. We aim to strengthen parliamentary democracy and encourage greater public involvement in politics. At the heart of our work is the principle that civic society is most effective when its citizens are connected with the institutions and individuals who represent them in the democratic process. There has never been more urgency for Parliament to engage with the public'.

40–43 Chancery Lane,
London
WC2A 1JA
Tel: 020 7438 1222
Email: hansard@hansard.lse.ac.uk
Web page: www.hansard-society.org.uk

Hansard has been associated with research and development of citizenship education and matters related to it for a number of decades. It funded a very important piece of work in the 1970s to do with political education in which Bernard Crick was a key figure. This work influenced David Blunkett who would later become the Education Secretary of State and would introduce citizenship education into the National Curriculum. It has many very valuable initiatives including resources on citizenship education, a clear focus on digital democracy and a large number of resources and ways into the study of politics. It is active at all main political party conferences.

IDEA 38

Oxfam

'Oxfam is a vibrant global movement of passionate, dedicated people fighting poverty together. Doing amazing work, together. People power drives everything we do. From saving lives and developing projects that put poor people in charge of their lives and livelihoods, to campaigning for change that lasts. That's Oxfam in action'.Oxfam House, 274 Banbury Rd, Oxford OX2 7DZ

Tel: 0870 333 2700

Web page: www.oxfam.org.uk/contact/index.htm

Oxfam has three main areas of work: emergency response ('People need help in an emergency – fast. We save lives, swiftly delivering aid, support and protection; and we help communities develop the capacity to cope with future crises'); development work ('Poor people can take control, solve their own problems, and rely on themselves – with the right support. We fund long-term work to fight poverty in thousands of communities worldwide'.); and, campaigning for change ('Poverty isn't just about lack of resources. In a wealthy world it's about bad decisions made by powerful people. Oxfam campaigns hard, putting pressure on leaders for real lasting change').

Oxfam is involved in a very wide range of issues and has produced extensive resources. Some of its extensive education resources may be seen at www.oxfam.org.uk/education/. Cool Planet, which is aimed directly at teachers, brings a global dimension to the classroom. The site contains resources for the classroom and links to citizenship related news.

The Carnegie Foundation is based in the USA and details of some of its educational work can be seen at: www.carnegiefoundation.org/

The UK base of the Foundation can be discovered at: www.carnegieuktrust.org.uk/

The Carnegie UK Trust investigates areas of public concern to influence policy and practice, in the interest of democracy, civil society and social justice.

Carnegie funds research and works in practical ways with schools and young people in other settings. Although much of its work is not principally focused on education it is a very significant organization for citizenship. A recent publication, ***Making good society***, which is the final report of the Commission of Inquiry into the Future of Civil Society, argues that civil society has been pushed to the margins in key areas including politics, finance and the media and that this must change. The report explores how civil society activity can help: grow a more civil economy; enable a rapid and just transition to a low carbon economy; democratize media ownership and content; and grow participatory and deliberative democracy.

IDEA

40

National Children's Bureau

'NCB is the leading national charity which supports children, young people and families and those who work with them. Our vision is a society in which children and young people are valued, their rights respected and responsibilities enhanced; our mission, to advance the well-being of children and young people across every aspect of their lives'.

8 Wakley Street, London EC1V 7QE

Tel: 020 7843 6000

Email: enquiries@ncb.org.uk

Web page: www.ncb.org.ukNCB provides the latest information on policy, research and best practice to support those working with and on behalf of children, young people, their families and carers.

NCB is one of the leading publishers in the field of children's services and children's studies as well as a key provider of professional development, running more than 70 conferences and training events each year.

NCB membership offers a practical and valuable resource for everyone who works with and for children and young people. Members receive a wide range of benefits to help them stay up to date with the latest news and opinion in the sector.

IDEA

41

School Councils UK

'School Councils UK is an educational charity which is recognized as Britain's most experienced training and support agency in the area of school and class councils. It has been helping schools to develop into caring communities working with teachers and pupils in primary secondary and special schools for over ten years. School Councils UK developed out of successful adult and youth councils created by the charity Priority Area Development (PAD) in some of the most deprived neighbourhoods in Liverpool.'

The Old Dairy, Victoria Street, Felixstowe IP11 7EW
Tel: 0845 456 9428
Email: sallypage@schoolcouncils.org
Web page: www.schoolcouncils.org

School councils, as shown later in this book, are a good way to promote active involvement by students and this charity provides an excellent background as to how school councils can be used to excellent effect in schools. As such they can play a key role in the development of citizenship education.

SECTION 6

What Can I Do to Promote the Following . . .?

IDEA 42

'A politically literate person will know what the main political disputes are about; what beliefs the main contestants have of them; how they are likely to affect him (sic) and he will have a predisposition to try to do something about it in a manner at once effective and respectful of the sincerity of others. Put another way, the teaching should help to develop empathy about other political viewpoints and to give people a knowledge of the actual political conflicts of the day; some language or system or concepts with which to express themselves critically about these problems and neither to expect too much or too little from their own action' (Crick, B. and Porter, A. (1978), *Political Education and Political Literacy*. London: Longman).

There are so many examples of excellent political literacy activities that it is difficult to refer only to a limited number. I think that they key is to recognize that civics (as information about political systems) is important but that it should be kept firmly in its place. The politics of everyday life – issues about power in the school, the local community, the world – are very important. The island game is a well-known way of introducing often very young children to systems of governments and key political concepts. In essence it involves asking students to imagine that they have been shipwrecked on a desert island and then asking them to consider who they would want to be in charge: the strongest/bravest/most intelligent? And would that person(s) be chosen by all or some or decided by some sort of contest? Difficult notions associated with democracy, oligarchy and dictatorship are normally explored by all students within a very short time. Another way to proceed is through dilemmas. Huddleston, in an excellent pack of political literacy materials, (*Citizens and Society*, Hodder and Stoughton) have used a summary of Ibsen's 'enemy of the people' to ask how politicians should respond to the media when it has been discovered that a problem has developed with a town's water supply.

Other examples of political literacy work can be seen elsewhere in this book in, for example, the sections on school councils, Number 10 Downing Street, and so on.

One example developed from the work of Lawrence Kohlberg is shown below. More can be read about the (rather controversial) levels of thinking that Kohlberg proposed. Ask the students to read the following dilemma and then answer the questions that follow:

A Story and a Question for Pupils

> A person was near death from a special kind of cancer. There was one drug that doctors thought might save the person. It was a form of radium that a druggist in the same town had recently discovered. The drug was expensive to produce, but the druggist was charging ten times what the drug had cost to make. The sick person's friend, Alex, went to other people to borrow the money, but could only get half of the price. Alex told the druggist that the friend was dying and asked for it to be sold cheaper or allow for payment to be made later. But the druggist said: 'No, I discovered the drug and I'm going to make money from it'. So Alex got desperate and broke into the druggist's store to steal the drug for the sick person.

Would you steal the drug to save your friend's life?

Questions/issues to consider:

1) Introducing the work to pupils

How would you introduce this activity to pupils? Would you explain the purpose of the exercise?

2) Teaching the main part of the lesson

Would you lead the exercise with the whole class; would pupils work in small groups; would pupils need to record decisions in writing (or some combination of these approaches)?

3) Drawing conclusions

Do you say that some pupils have reached the right answer? Do you refer to levels of thinking? Do all pupils get to see the levels that you and/or Kohlberg recommend at the end of the exercise?

4) General reflections

Kohlberg suggested that higher level thinking involves recognition of key principles to do with justice; lower levels involve a simple recognition of the existence of rules or laws and a desire to avoid punishment. What do you think?

Ask students to undertake this role play:

Leafy Lane Primary School (LLPS) pupils are looking forward to going to Good Results Comprehensive School (GRCS). LLPS is in a village or suburb based 4 miles away from the highly regarded GRCS. A link has existed between the schools for 30 years. GRCS is already oversubscribed and new housing is planned.

The local council feels that Good Results Comprehensive has too many pupils. It also sees that other local schools, especially Town Comprehensive (TC), would benefit from attracting more pupils. TC does not achieve results similar to those at GRCS. TC is situated in a fairly pleasant area but with many more social problems than the areas that feed into GRCS. It is suggested that children in the LLPS area should in future feed into TC.

A local action group is started by parents of LLPS. They demand that their link with GRCS is maintained. Many teachers at GRCS believe in the value of comprehensive education and feel that GRCS may be developing into a school that selects by post code. Some distrust the local council, suspecting that financial issues are governing decision-making. Some are wondering about the impact of changing catchment areas on the nature of the school and the results that can be achieved in the future.

A campaign group (perhaps assisted by parents) is quickly formed by school students. The Council is accused in a press release of 'social engineering'. Students, acting independently from teachers, organize a letter writing campaign to local councillors which focuses on the negative attributes of TC. A local council meeting is disrupted by shouting from students from GRCS. Two student members of the school council (representatives of year 7 and year 11) propose that the council pass a motion to support the actions of those who have written the letters.

Students can be asked: ‘how does this specific issue and the more general matter of community involvement relate to citizenship education’:

1. what arguments about citizenship were put forward?
2. what characterizes a good (and less good) argument?

IDEA

45

Group Discussions

Citizenship is characterized by positive, active, knowledgeable participation. Perhaps one of the most obvious ways in which that involvement can be generated is through discussion. Much of the work on discussions derives from a concern with identifying the inputs that can be made by individuals. In order to extend this sort of work it might be worth looking for ways to explore what can be gained from group discussions. Many interesting and valuable interactions can occur if people are asked to discuss a challenging problem in collaborative ways. An example of such a problem adapted from Plous (1993) is as follows: 'a man bought a chair for £60 and sold it for £70. Then he bought it back for £80 and sold it for £90. How much profit did he make'? Quite a lot of useful discussion can take place around the ways in which the group operates to come to a decision: does one person dominate; do all voices carry equal weight, etc. The above example has been chosen because it normally leads to a rapid response from an individual. It then requires another individual to intercede with a different answer before discussion leads to a resolution. When another, more value laden scenario is used one can begin to reveal many more issues (and, probably more valuable matters). If we ask a question in certain ways it is likely to prompt a particular immediate answer. A question such as: 'do you think that people who don't work should be paid?' often leads to an immediate and sharp negative. But after a few moments others will ask about who is involved, why they are not working, how much support they will receive and from whom and for how long. Groups can, at times, not be the best decision making arenas but it is important to explore what happens within them.

IDEA

46

Presentation Skills: Deciding When to Speak

There are various comments in this book about presentation skills. Here I intend to focus only on one specific issue. When should people speak and when should they keep quiet? If students have a good idea when is the best time to introduce it? Should they seize the moment and speak as soon as a relevant thought pops into their head? Should they risk waiting until they have thought things through and risk the meeting moving onto other business? In many ways this issue is linked to the idea shown above (idea 38) about group discussions.

A decision about when to speak is relevant to making contributions to debates. If citizenship is concerned, at least in part, with making one's voice heard then it is very useful to help students develop an ability to contribute to debates. Some would argue that speaking first allows one to set the agenda before people become bored or confused. Others suggest that a decision to speak last means that one can use the ideas of the people who have spoken before you and you have the opportunity to leave the audience with your ideas ringing in their heads. Occasionally, it is best to wait until other speakers are exhausted by debate and actively want the solution that a late entrant to a debate can supply. There is probably no single best way to proceed especially as these matters are so dependent upon particular contexts. However, one review of research suggests:

> if you are offered the chance to speak first or last in a public debate, you should speak first if the other side will follow you immediately and there will be a delay in the debate and people's responses to it. For example, if you are debating an issue that will be voted on in a week, then you should choose to speak first. On the other hand, if some time will separate the two communications, and if people will be asked to act immediately after the second presentation, you should capitalize on the 'regency effect' and choose to go last. (Plous 1993, 44)

IDEA

47

Understanding Bias

If citizenship involves discussion and debate students will need to be able to show some sophistication in their analysis of one-sided presentations. At times people can be persuaded that something looks better than it really is. Does this mean that when presentations are being made people should be encouraged not only to listen to what is being said, but also think about the context in which it is being said and the ways in which it is being presented? In this section some issues are raised about political communication.

Contrasting images: a presenter may decide to talk about a bad thing before she discusses the policy or idea that is being introduced. Occasionally, estate agents are accused of this sort of tactic by showing a very expensive property or a run-down property before they 'reveal' the house that they really want to sell. It is very easy to model this sort of approach by using estate agents' literature on two properties.

Making more of your track record than is really justified: if a teacher or student wants to persuade others to agree with something, do they spend a great deal of time talking not about the issue at hand but about successes that occurred elsewhere?

Using factual information selectively: when a person wants to present a case that seems 'solid' hard data may be used but what is being omitted? The easy example here would be the report of a football game where a team scored 10 goals (the fact that the opposing team scored 12 is omitted). Similar things can be done with statistics ('there has been a 100 per cent increase in . . .' could mean that one more person has been involved).

Using emotional language: what sort of emotional appeals do politicians make? This relates to the selection of key words and also to general appeals to things that cannot be easily disputed (need to do one's best; love one's family; love one's country, etc.).

KEY TEXT:

For an interesting discussion about political communication including matters not presented here such as body language and audience response, see Bull, P. (2003), *The microanalysis of political communication: claptrap and ambiguity*. London: Routledge.

IDEA

48

Participation

Participation is the principal but elusive goal of many who are involved in citizenship education, but what does it mean? It is a challenging area that should explicitly inform all the work that is done in citizenship education.

Levels of participation (taken from Roger Hart (1992), *Children's participation: the theory and practice of involving young citizens in community development and environmental care*. London: Earthscan.) can be seen as follows:

1. Manipulation. Children are engaged or used for the benefit of their own interests, formulated by adults, while the children themselves do not understand the implications.
2. Decoration. Children are called in to embellish adult actions. Adults, do not, however, pretend that all this is in the interest of the children themselves.
3. Tokenism. Children are apparently given a voice, but this is to serve the child friendly image adults want to create, rather than the interest of the children themselves.
4. Assigned but informed. Adults take the initiative to call in children, but inform them on how and why. Only after the children have come to understand the intentions of the project and the point of their involvement do the children decide whether or not to take part.
5. Consulted and informed. Children are intensively consulted on a project designed and run by adults.
6. Adult initiated, shared decisions with children. In the case of projects concerned with community development, initiators such as policy makers, community workers and local residents frequently involve various interest groups and age groups.
7. Child initiated and directed. Children conceive, organize and direct a project themselves without adult interference.
8. Child initiated, shared decisions with adults.

Ask students to review situations with which they are familiar in school and indicate the number in the above list that could be applied. Teachers will know the situations that can realistically be identified for discussion (the school itself or distance the discussion by, for example, talking about the local council, the relationship between voters and the government, the input that is possible in imaginary families, etc.).

Citizenship explores and promotes inclusion (for children of all abilities). Jerome Bruner was right when he argued a long time ago that it is possible to focus on valid concepts with all learners and that to avoid doing so would be to practise an unacceptable form of exclusion. What needs to be changed is not the concept that is to be learned but rather the way in which it is explored. This means that the lessons that we would teach with all learners are suitable for those with special educational needs as long as we have paid appropriate attention to language level, the amount of material to be used and the level of independence to be experienced by learners. Lee Jerome has written good material in which he recommends that attention be paid to differentiation through use of resources, classroom layout, language, teaching approaches, etc.

It is possible to consider developing work for citizenship by planning along three dimensions: responsibility (there should be less direction for those who have the potential to chart their own routes); knowledge (expectations about the amount that is known should be much greater); reflection (there should be a sense in which responses are nuanced rather than superficially generalized and also that diverse threads of an argument or issue can be pulled together). The ideas given above should underpin all good teaching.

There are very many general resources (see www.teachernet.gov.uk/wholeschool/sen/). The Institute for Citizenship's site (see www.citizen.org.uk/SENResources.htm) and the Citizenship Foundation's site (see www.citizenshipfoundation.org.uk/main/resource.php?y17) contain some interesting resources which are particularly related to citizenship education.

KEY TEXT:

Fergusson, A. and Lawson, H. (2003), *Access to Citizenship: Curriculum planning and practical activities for pupils with learning difficulties.* London: David Fulton.

SECTION 7

What Can I Do to Teach Citizenship Through . . .?

IDEA

50

History

There are many who have asserted that the connections between history and citizenship are very strong. The well-known quotation 'politics is present history; history is past politics' illustrates the matter nicely. There should be a recognizable citizenship element (of which students are explicitly aware) that normally reveals itself through a link between the past and contemporary society and a focus on the sort of concept (such as power) that is essentially about citizenship and history. There should be, at least within the classroom, some sort of active participation by school students. These things are vitally important. The key is not to rely merely on content – Ofsted has criticized those teachers who do the standard lesson on the suffragettes and then say, without really understanding why, that it is also a citizenship lesson.

Ask students to look at certain features of the past that are part of our contemporary society and suggest what they reveal about our ideas today. Organize a thought shower (or, just simply present a list) of special days that are commemorated, place names and symbols. Research their origins and suggest their current meanings. Waterloo station, Trafalgar Square, 'Land of hope and glory' and the Union Jack could be included as well as others such as United Nations Day, the flag of the European Union and the right to vote for 18 year olds. Two key questions would be used: what is the history behind this idea/practice/place? What does it tell us about life in Britain today? This can help students enquire and communicate and, if they investigate actively, begin to participate responsibly in contemporary debates about identity they will be engaged in citizenship education.

KEY TEXT:

Arthur, J. et al. (2001), *Citizenship through Secondary History*. London: Routledge.

Davies, I. (ed.) (2011), *Debates in History Teaching*. Abingdon, UK: Routledge.

The politics of place is a very important way of understanding contemporary society. Who lives where is for many people a very obvious citizenship-type question. One idea for classroom work would be to choose something from the local area and ask students to explore why it has appeared or why and how it has happened. Take a map of two contrasting suburbs (real or imagined; close to the school or from another part of the country depending on the issues that you think can be raised with your students). Provide, or ask students to research, some background information (examples of estate agents' information about houses in the two areas; crime rate; examination results achieved by local schools; number of people unemployed, etc.). Highlight (or ask students to identify) certain features on the map such as hospital, schools, leisure centres, transport routes and shops. Then ask the pupils to draw up a list of factors that might have led to people living in one or the other of these areas (they will perhaps mention: economic factors such as closeness to place of work, house prices; personal factors such as location of family or friends; environmental factors such as desire to be in the countryside or city; there may be other factors to do with political or cultural issues). Finally, a discussion could occur about the distribution of scarce goods that is occurring in these different contexts. Another similar exercise could be based, loosely, on town planning in which students are asked to develop their own ideas about what could and should be provided in a local area. These ideas can be extended to include global and environmental issues.

KEY TEXT:

Lambert, D. and Machon, P. (2001), *Citizenship through Secondary Geography*. London: Routledge. Look also at the web sites of the Geographical Association and the Royal Geographical Society.

IDEA 52

English

There are many connections between language and power, between stories and culture and communication and social issues. It is good to keep up to date through NATE (National Association for Teaching English), EAL (English as an additional language) initiatives, etc. There is a very close link to English in the skills element of the citizenship curriculum (e.g. how to express an opinion in writing and verbally).

Ask your students to analyze the ways in which a politician answers questions by watching a brief excerpt from a televised interview. They should focus on:

1. body language;
2. length of answer;
3. number and type of interruptions (by interviewer or interviewee);
4. use of factual information;
5. use of emotional language;
6. explanations of what has been done in the past;
7. promises of what will be done in the future;
8. personal statements that might be used to gain support;
9. negative statements about self or others;
10. positive statements about self or others.

Another example of an activity that could take place in an English lesson and used for citizenship education could be letter writing in order to make specific points to particular audiences. Devise a brief scenario which leads to the need for a written complaint. Ask students to compose such a letter considering what is put in the first and last sentence and paragraph (these are usually the spaces for summary statements); what sort of evidence is used in the letter; what sort of language (detached, formal or emotional?); to whom should it be addressed? Some students could also analyze the differences between submissions that might be made to a broadsheet compared to those to a tabloid newspaper.

KEY TEXT:

Moss, J. (2001), *Citizenship through Secondary English* London: Routledge.

IDEA

53

Science

Science GCSE syllabuses emphasize the value of science for citizens. The Wellcome Trust has funded initiatives in which science and citizenship are explored and the Association for Science Education has promoted generally context-based approaches to science. There is a great deal of interest in the ways that young people can develop social and political understanding and action. At times we need to be a little cautious (context-based teaching is occasionally just a way of using exciting citizenship content to teach what would otherwise be a rather dry topic).

Very many valuable school projects can easily be suggested: a joint geography and science exploration of the siting of a nuclear energy station or the advantages and disadvantages of renewal energy (there are currently a number of enquiries into wind farms that can provide a lot of classroom material). You could set up a science 'media watch' in which stories are identified and assessed for their science content with assessments being made for what is being claimed (what is said to be true; what is said to be harmful; what is said to require further investigation). The important thing is to keep asking 'where's the citizenship'? – students need to have knowledge about contemporary society, understanding of citizenship concepts (e.g. power) and be able to learn about participation.

KEY TEXT:

Fullick, P. and Ratcliffe, M. (eds) (1996), *Teaching Ethical Aspects of Science*, Southhampton, UK: Bassett Press.

Levinson, R. and Reiss, M. J. (eds) (2003), *Key Issues in Bioethics: a guide for teachers*. London: RoutledgeFalmer.

Ratcliffe, M. and Grace, M. (2003), *Science Education for Citizenship*. Maidenhead, Berkshire: Open University Press.

There is a strong connection between art and society. Try some of the following activities:

1. students are asked to study examples of propaganda posters and to draw their own. They should label the things that they feel make their poster effective (e.g. striking colour; strong attractive central image; effective caption; deliberate attempt to appeal to individuals and/or specific groups; emphasis of the need for action, probably in light of an external threat). Students should be asked whether propaganda is necessarily a bad thing. Students could reflect on how they can identify the difference between reliable images and propaganda.
2. Students create a picture of the local/regional/global community. What is emphasized and why? What has been drawn as an attempt at realism and what is shown idealistically? What real objects have been included and what items are there as symbols.
3. Students draw three self-portraits. One will be an attempt at an accurate realist description; another will be obviously 'modern' in which only symbols will be used; the final picture will be a blend between the real and the 'modern'. What is being shown and to what extent do these portraits tell us about citizenship today. (Some will emphasize technology, sport in the community, connections with or isolation from others and so on).
4. Students explore a case study of the work of one picture or one artist that was obviously involved with political matters. An examination of Guernica by Picasso could work well. This could form the basis of some interesting cross-departmental work with history.
5. For older students, questions about morality and toleration can be raised by looking at the work of certain artists. Robert Mapplethorpe is an obvious example (but this will be far too 'strong' for most schools and perhaps someone like Chris Offili's use

of animal dung in portraits would be easier – choose your controversial artist with care!)

6. Investigate the establishment of a new art gallery. There have been very many in recent years (e.g. the Baltic in Newcastle; Tate in Liverpool, etc.). How much public money has been spent? How would students judge value for money? What is the benefit for citizens?

Show students a 10 minute extract from the 'last night of the proms' and then ask them to:

1. analyze the lyrics of Land of Hope and Glory. What messages are being conveyed;
2. think about whether the music has an effect on the listeners and if so, what that might be (is it sensible to talk about music itself being patriotic or is this meaning given by the listeners);
3. analyze the behaviour of the audience. What are they doing? Why? Is this acceptable as a warm hearted celebration of our country or is it likely to offend some people (is it aggressive; xenophobic, etc.).

Ask students to consider the case study of Shostakovich's 5th symphony. Ask students to listen to the music without knowing anything about it. Then supply some background. The Russian composer had written an opera called Lady Macbeth of Mtsensk. This had been interpreted as an attack on Stalin and on the communist system. A strongly worded criticism of that music was published in 1936 in the official newspaper, Pravda (the word Pravda means 'truth'). Some say that Shostakovich then wrote his 5th symphony in order to apologize. The subtitle that is often used for the 5th symphony is *'A Soviet artist's reply to just criticism'*. This was not Shostakovich's own subtitling, but apparently suggested by a journalist. Some say that the composer actually intended the 5th to be a further critique of communism. Ask students to listen again – what do they think and what would they have to do in order to find out more? Perhaps look at the composer's diary, letters; investigate the official reaction was to the 5th; investigate how audiences reacted. The students should be asked to consider whether music itself has a meaning relevant to citizenship and whether they are likely to be significant differences between the intention of the composer and reactions to his work. More broadly, students should be asked to think about the relationship between government and art – should the former control the latter and if so how and by how much? (Good material exists on Youtube that would allow teachers to show extracts from the symphony and there are presentations about Shostakovich's life with the music as background).

Maths is not objective knowledge but just as culturally determined as other subjects. Ethnomathematics explores our reliance on what is essentially an Arabic heritage of mathematical understanding. If citizenship is, at least in part, about understanding power then this sort of awareness about how we come to accept certain ideas is very relevant.

The skills of maths can be developed in real life situations that are generally relevant to citizenship. One cannot work out income tax, the change that should be received in a shop, fair shares for three people, etc., if one does not have some basic mathematical or arithmetical knowledge and understanding.

Direct use of maths for citizenship purposes can be explored. When a school has undertaken a mock election the maths department can help count the votes, show the extent of any 'swing', the proportions of people who have voted, and what would have happened if a variety of systems had been used (first past the post as opposed to single transferable vote). Using Spearman's rank, students can be asked if preferences for different political parties are erratic or consistent when considered over several themes such as health, education and defence. Work on probability could be done in relation to voting patterns during the last few decades. It is easy to obtain figures about the extent to which different age groups have voted during the last few general elections. On the basis of these figures how likely is it that more than 50 per cent of the 18–24 will vote in the next general election and how does this relate to the actual result? Work on averages, modes and medians would explain the health of individual businesses or the whole economy during periods of office of different governments (and then the claims made by politicians can be investigated). Use of actual figures, proportions and percentages can be quite interesting in helping young people to understand debates about migration.

IDEA 57

Religious Education

If citizenship education is in part concerned with ensuring that young people are prepared for life in a democratic, pluralistic, multifaith society then religious education (RE) is centrally important for organizing the development of that subject.

I will mention only three ideas that can be used:

1. A series of weddings shown in role plays involving students as the principal characters followed by questions and debates: what, according to the different individuals and groups involved, is the purpose of marriage; what is the link between theology and social convention (are there any consistencies and inconsistencies); who has the power to make decisions at crucial points in the process; who currently is excluded from wedding ceremonies (this principally applies to the gay community who can now take part in civil partnerships) and is this acceptable; given the rate of divorce is marriage now an outdated concept? Research about one or more communities could be followed by a role play (e.g. of a marriage) and small group discussions focussed on the key questions mentioned above.
2. A visit to a local graveyard or cemetery can lead to much valuable work on identity and power. What symbols are being used on the graves; does the cemetery reflect the nature of the local population or does this link with geography not apply; what do the graves tell us about the religious beliefs of that community, etc.
3. Case studies can be developed to explore the link between citizenship and religious practice. For example, the decision by the French government to ban the wearing of religious symbols in schools, and also the last few decades of history in Northern Ireland supply rich data for investigation. The visits of key figures (e.g. the visit of the Pope in 2010) can be a useful starting point to explore the nature of the interaction between what could be called social views (e.g. about the role of women) and theology.

The processes of physical education (PE) can be enormously relevant to citizenship education. One only has to think of the caricature of the games teacher in the film *Kes* to know how one can easily work against the values of citizenship.

A lot of nonsense is written about the so-called determination of trendy teachers to abandon competition and insist only on collaborative games (one high profile commentator implying that education is now locked into some sort of Alice in Wonderland phase, has sneered at the supposed notion that 'all must have prizes'). But co-operation is important. Competition and collaboration are not polar opposites and students can easily be alerted to the sorts of team work that is required before victory (either in terms of good sporting behaviour) or in the sense of winning against another team. PE teachers have a good deal to teach us in how they decide to organize skill based sessions. But be careful – just organizing a team game is not necessarily citizenship education.

Health education can be a key feature of citizenship education if it is considered in a societal – rather than merely a personal – context. PE teachers can tell us about the best ways in which a healthy body can be created and preserved. It is, normally, only in the examination courses related to PE that the issues associated with individual health and the wider society can be probed explicitly and in-depth. But those issues are very important indeed: what connections exist between the tax to be paid to the National Health Service and the responsibility for all citizens to maintain a healthy level of fitness; what links exist between diet, health and the pressures that emerge from a free society in which advertising is a normal part of commercial activity; to what extent should the government impose health? All teachers can, in a positive way, encourage some sort of reflection upon these matters.

IDEA 59

Innovative designs are successful only when there is acceptance that there will be a direct positive impact on society. The link with citizenship is therefore very clear as it is a political – as well as a simple design – issue to decide what should be regarded as a positive technological development. The days are long gone of students producing a cake slice for the purpose of filling low status lesson time and providing parents with a moment of pride. Assessing need, developing an idea practically so that something may be made, testing and refining a prototype and producing the final version that will be subjected to a rigorous evaluation by users are the normal procedures that drive many lessons. Many examples could be given of successful work, but I will give only one instance here (which is based on a real event). A student visited a vet's surgery to investigate the possibilities of creating a new design. A long process eventually resulted in a design and manufacture of a device that would hold open a dog's mouth during surgery. The value of such work was clear for the design and technology teacher and the citizenship element would be met by the determination of you and students to ask challenging questions about the ethical procedures required, and questions about who set these parameters and whether they could be altered. These ethical procedures included asking questions about the relationship between vet and customer and animal. Broader questions could be asked about whether the use of materials was environmentally appropriate; if the idea could or should be commercially exploited (and if so who would stand to benefit); whether the development of surgical appliances for animals represents the best use of time for all involved; and, what sort of transferable skills were developed.

Learning a language involves a uniquely valuable insight into very many cultural issues. There is an obvious determination on the part of language students to understand the 'other' and as such there is rich potential for citizenship education.

Three ideas spring to mind:

1. collaborative projects to investigate by e-mail discussion the ways in which people live today. A little more ambition is involved if a contemporary controversial issue is chosen that reflects different opinions within the country being studied and perhaps involves different perspectives between the home country of the students and the country in which the foreign language is spoken. This focus on controversial issues can also be done in collaboration with another department. There are many opportunities to work with, for example the history department (e.g. how do young Germans think about the contemporary significance of the Holocaust; what do Spanish students think about the Armada, etc.). At all times, but especially when working with another department, it is very important to keep the citizenship focus clearly in mind;
2. exploring the meaning of extracts from relevant literature (e.g. the work of Lorca, Camus, and – perhaps only for the really ambitious even if just using extracts – what are we told about justice morality and responsibility by *Crime and Punishment*). There are very few novels that do not have a political element insofar as they are about society as well as individuals within a narrative;
3. during an exchange programme arrange for investigations to take place into local or national issues (e.g. an exchange with a school in the Loire Valley could lead to work on the relationship between wine, health and the French economy, or, alternatively, a debate about the siting of nuclear power stations in areas of natural beauty).

IDEA 61

Business Studies

Business and enterprise education schemes are full of potential for work on citizenship. Only a few examples can be given here.

1. Marketing: a colleague of mine used to do an exercise called 'sniffing out stereotypes'. He would ask boys if they would wear perfume and the girls if they would wear aftershave. Obvious strongly phrased responses were achieved! Then he would show adverts from glossy magazines about male and female scents. The obvious targeting of the adverts was analyzed. Finally, he would invite students to identify the male and female scents by sniffing separate but not labelled cotton wool balls kept in small glass jars that had been sprayed with different products. Students were often unable to identify what was male and what was female. The difference was in the idea rather than the product. Similar things can be done by looking at the words used to advertise products, judging to what extent the potential customer is being sold an image. (An example of this from a very long time ago is the advert for Martini – the taste is never mentioned while we focus on images of style – 'the right one, the bright one').
2. Human resource management: students can be invited to go through a selection process – identifying a job; writing a letter of application; attending an interview. Throughout they will be asked to focus on the (fictional) characteristics and their individual performance. But they will also be asked to consider broader issues: what sort of balance does the employer and society wish to achieve across the workforce (would it matter if every employee was white male?)
3. Business Plans: students could be asked to develop a plan concentrating on the product, anticipated start-up costs, profits, unique selling point and customer profile. Groups of students acting as owners, investors, potential employees and potential customers are asked to develop and/or review the plan. It is likely

that market positioning will prove to be important (the ideas of Michael Porter could be useful here see http://en.wikipedia.org/wiki/Michael_Porter).

As always, the key thing is to ensure a high profile for the citizenship issue: in the above cases equality, ethics and socially acceptable competition are relevant ideas.

Many schools have a modular system in which citizenship education is taught within or as part of a Personal and Social Education (PSE) framework. There are several challenges here:

1. The characterization of PSE varies hugely – PSHE; PSHCE (where the 'C' means 'culture' or 'community'); PSHCCE (to include citizenship). This may betray insecurity. History lessons are just titled 'history'. We don't feel the need to give a title that makes clear the political, social, economic and cultural features of the history curriculum, so why should we spell things out in other areas?;
2. More important, there are very complex debates about the nature of the overlap between the personal and the political. Perhaps traditional politics (or civics) which emphasizes constitutional structures is not immediately personal. But newer forms of politics – feminism, community activism, antiracism are often directly dependent on personal factors.

It is vital to ensure that there is a clear understanding of the nature of citizenship and that this is communicated easily to students. Citizenship, of course, involves personal factors but it is essentially a public matter. This means that when we examine issues in citizenship lessons there is a need for a public focus. At times, content is less important than how it is used.

For example:

1. A PSE lesson will examine smoking. Why do individuals smoke (peer pressure) and what happens to his or her body when they do? Powerful – and very necessary – lessons can help individuals to realize the dangers of smoking;
2. A citizenship lesson will also investigate smoking but with a different focus. It would be useful to refer to some of the personal factors that lead to some people smoking and to look at the effects on those

individuals. But that is by and large motivational or introductory material. The key in a citizenship lesson is to look at smoking in a public context. How many people in the country/local area/world smoke? What sort of people are they (men/women/rich/poor)? Why do they smoke (advertising and cultural factors including views based on what a 'real' man is like, such as the 'Marlboro Man'). What public advantages and disadvantages are there (taxation/public health, etc.) when the population smokes? What are the limits to governmental action – should all smokers be punished? Parallels can be drawn here with prohibition of alcohol in the USA in the 1920s and 1930s and with the fight against drugs today.

SECTION 8

Whole School Approaches

IDEA

63

Charitable Activity

It is enormously difficult to discuss charitable activity without giving the misleading impression that one is suggesting going back to earlier and unhelpful versions of citizenship education in which young people were expected merely to act, to step in, where the welfare state was failing. I also do not want to include one charity over another (although other specific charities have already been mentioned in this book and one is highlighted below in this section). Key questions for students and teachers include: do we have responsibility for others (and if so who?); what are the problems (as well as the benefits) of charitable donations; what sort of links can be made between charitable work and global and environmental issues; how can we support charitable work and at the same time portray the developing world as richly diverse (and not inadvertently giving the false impression that charity just involves rich people giving money to people who have failed)?

In light of the above I would like to give one example of a charity that could be explored. Giving Nation is a project that provides paper resources and activities for schools. Their web site is: www.g-nation.co.uk/teachers/ G-Week is a nationwide celebration of giving in schools. It provides an opportunity to recognize pupils' achievements for charity and community.

The titles of their classroom resources are shown below:

Charitable activity:

1. what is charity? Charities and charity – the who and the why
2. who wants to change the world? – charity as a power for transformation
3. how do charities spend the money we give them? – how charities work in practice
4. how do you decide which charities to support? – publicity and promotion: how would you do it?

5. action planning – numbers and skills needed to make a change Volunteering
6. what is volunteering
7. the benefits of volunteering

IDEA

64

Action Groups

In a sense all those involved in citizenship education are part of an action group. They want to make something happen. However, there is of course a difference between the sort of activity that allows people to develop knowledge and skills for the purpose of exploring key issues and eventually deciding what they will do; and, on the other hand, promoting a particular outcome that might be deemed to have political connotations. The latter is normally to be avoided, although there are some who claim that citizenship education can only be meaningful as it emerges from involvement in real political processes. We need also to be aware that seeming to be inactive – think of Gandhi's passive resistance, and perhaps also knowledgeable voters who show their disapproval of the governing party by not voting – can be as important a feature of citizenship as more obviously doing things. Finally, I think it is important to stress that in educational contexts reflection (in which people consider difficult questions such as why did I take part?; should others have taken part as well?; did my involvement make things better or worse?; what evidence am I using as I develop answers to these questions?) is a vitally important part of the process. Participation itself is ultimately, in my view, in school contexts not the most important factor but rather what people learn from that participation. Of course, it will be important if people are allowed the opportunity to learn that they are capable through their involvement in real situations.

It is possible and quite common for schools to establish local branches of organizations such as Amnesty International or Greenpeace. A less ambitious option would be simply to review several web sites with perhaps an invitation to a few speakers that might help clarify issues about participation. What do they find positive or helpful and what really gets in the way of their work? It would be important to establish a balanced programme if speakers are invited to the school.

Many organizations are interested in helping schools work together. This should be done in the spirit of positive collaboration as an aspect of global citizenship education: some sort of paternalistic 'do-gooding' will not help. The British Council, European Union, Oxfam, Action Aid and many others are available to work with teachers. Government departments may also be helpful. The Department for International Development (see www.dfid.gov.uk/Getting-Involved/For-schools/), for example, facilitates global partnerships between schools and also helps to run global conferences for students.

Good work can be undertaken electronically without ever leaving the classroom. But if one can be ambitious, exchange schemes have the power to change lives. I have been involved with schemes that allowed teachers and students to make links with many different countries for teachers, student teachers and school students. There are, of course, problems that must be overcome dealing with resources and ensuring that the requirements of the home institution's programme can be met while individuals are abroad as well as the many 'everyday' matters to do with personal safety and security of identity. Of course, issues of national and global citizenship become very apparent when one attempts to move learners from one country to another. A critical but positive approach should be developed so that learners do not merely marvel at the 'other'.

Many universities produce and have collections of resources about studying abroad. Browsing the web pages of Queen's University in Canada, for example, can be useful. The European Union facilitates the Comenius programme. Modern foreign language departments have, for many years, been involved in very valuable school exchanges (and it is hoped that finance, and the need for secure high-quality accommodation does not lead to a reduction in this work).

KEY TEXT:

Lewin, R. (ed.) (2009), *Handbook of practice and research in study abroad: higher education and the quest for global citizenship.* Abingdon, UK: Routledge. (A chapter in the book by Davies and Pike describes and discusses one project involving transatlantic exchange).

Peer mentoring is a system where individual students are identified as being able to assist others in the resolution of problems. This does not mean that it is a system of crisis management: it is much more positive and mainstream than that. At times, teachers simply select the mentors, arguing that they need to be sure that there is a diverse mix of students including, for example, younger and older, male and female. But many feel that the selection of the peer mentoring team should be left entirely to the student body itself and decided through the process of an election.

The mentors will need communication and conflict resolution skills and should be genuinely interested in raising the self-esteem of their peers and contributing to the improvement of the school ethos. The mentors will help the student voice to be heard. Training will be required for all those who take on the role.

There are different types of involvement including peer learning, peer mentoring (often for social issues) and conflict resolution. While it may be worthwhile for teachers to take responsibility for the training, this may be done by peers (especially if the scheme has been running for some time) and perhaps through the involvement of an outside agency. Various organizations exist to help offer training which may be suitable for staff and/or students (e.g. Mediation UK see admin@ukmediation.net).

Teachers and others need to be alert to the difficult issues that may arise. Misunderstandings may occur and it is not unusual for carers and others to express concern about the revelation of what might be regarded as confidential information during peer involvement. There needs to be careful (but not inappropriately intrusive) monitoring by staff and a clear organizational structure for what happens when concern is expressed.

KEY TEXT:

Some useful examples of peer mentoring are given in Clough, N. and Holden, C. (2002), *Education for Citizenship: ideas into action. A practical guide for teachers of pupils aged 7–14.* London: Routledge Falmer.

IDEA 67

Ethos

The combination of all the work suggested in this book, hopefully, is the way to establish an appropriate classroom and school climate or atmosphere or ethos. The achievement of this elusive goal is probably the acid test of citizenship education (but we should be honest and realistic and accept that an argument that a school 'delivers' its citizenship education programme entirely through ethos is probably just an excuse for no one really doing anything). Nevertheless, ethos is a key factor for citizenship education and moreover one that can be responsible for helping improve academic results (see Trafford 1993). It is important to remember that almost all major research reports on citizenship education indicate that effective classroom learning is dependent on an appropriate ethos.

It is for each school to decide upon their preferred ethos and work towards it. I do not believe that it is essential for democratic procedures to be in place before one can claim that an appropriate ethos has been achieved. Indeed, schools are never able to become democracies, and teachers, obviously, always need to show professional leadership. The key for staff is to be usefully authoritative without being authoritarian. The following gives an indication of what, according to one author, may be found in democratic schools (Fletcher 1989):

1. active critical school councils
2. fully participative staff in which they can shape the agenda
3. heads that are committed to emphasise principles not details, tirelessly 'explaining' the school and confidence in staff and others
4. parents that are regarded as partners with rights of open access to the school and elected to key positions
5. governors that are elected and discuss in a body where no single group holds an effective majority

KEY TEXT:

Fletcher, C. (1989), 'Democratisation on Trial', in K. Jensen and W. Walker (eds) *Towards Democratic Schooling: European Experiences*. Milton Keynes, Buckinghamshire: Open University.

Trafford, B. (1993), *Sharing Power in Schools: raising standards*. Ticknall, South Derbyshire: Education Now.

There is such a thing as society but, of course, it is probably better to recognize that within any community (local, national or global) there are different groups and sometimes fairly difficult tensions. It may be unwise to invite someone into the school for a brief question and answer session simply to pretend that there are good relations with the local community. Better, perhaps, to set up some sort of discussion or other activity (including, for example, linked recycling projects, reading schemes for the elderly or very young).

I have seen Question Times work very well in a project managed by the Institute for Citizenship. In these events, local schools were invited to prepare questions for an invited panel that would include young people but also a representative of the police, residents' group, local council and social services. The panel is usually subjected to a pretty intense informed grilling. With careful preparation and follow-up, these events can be very successful for the full school populations of all schools invited.

The following could be useful preparation for such an event:

1. careful research into a particular issue
2. help with the formulation of a question: it should be clear, brief, positively phrased and obviously a question rather than a statement
3. the initial question should be linked to a possible follow up question (so, if the answer is X then I can ask Y; if on the other hand the answer is A I can say B)
4. training in careful listening can be useful so that the question and answer and discussion can be analyzed later (were the questions answered; what sort of data were used; what sort of language – including body language – were used and so on).

David Dimbleby is president of the Institute for Citizenship and useful work can be done in the BBC Schools Question Time.

These can link with many of the activities that have been outlined in this book. For example, Question Time events, school council activities, arrangements for mock elections and much else can be focused through assemblies. Of course, other possibilities exist. A series of invited speakers can give a 10 minute talk on a particular theme. A teacher or student can give an account of what could be called 'issue (or thought) for the day' based on a topical news story.

A brief role play can take place to explore reactions to something in the school or local community that is currently regarded as problematic. For example, it is possible to present simple perennial issues, such as which year groups are asked to go into the dining room before others, to be considered from different viewpoints or, perhaps more challenging, a presentation with discussion around the decision of the local council to change a leisure centre into a hotel and casino.

The management of these events is crucial. There should be an opportunity for students to experience some success by showing off their knowledge and understanding, their ability to speak in public and the generation of a positive community spirit. The relationship between the teachers and the students is very important. The students must be supported and be given the chance to show their leadership skills (Hart's ladder of participation referred to elsewhere in this book is relevant here). The presentation of a poorly thought through case about a controversial topic which leads to disagreement and dissatisfaction is obviously counterproductive. The key citizenship concepts and the skills that are being developed should always be kept clearly in mind if the assembly is to be educationally worthwhile.

If genuine participation is not being practised (e.g. if students are merely listening to teachers lecturing them about the need to take part) then citizenship education is perhaps not taking place or at least the opportunities for citizenship are not being fully explored.

There are some dangers to avoid and some goals to aim for:

1. If we involve students, it should be done in a way that does not mean that they will be seen merely as 'agents' of the staff;
2. Any sort of pupil monitor (and monitoring) system may be seen negatively;
3. Make sure the individuals who are given special responsibilities are representative of the wider student body;
4. Development of the knowledge, skills and dispositions of the students charged with responsibility will need to be addressed (this means that there needs to be an explicit educational programme to allow for their development to occur);
5. The extent of their responsibilities should be made clear. They should not mistakenly imagine that they suddenly have responsibility to change the school overnight. If the principal responsibility is for them to be involved in a certain role at a particular point, then that needs to be stated; if the role is to be more wide-ranging, then that also needs to be stated;
6. The processes by which those charged with responsibilities are to engage with the wider student body should be clarified. Are they expected to consult through assemblies, staff meetings, be involved in staff appointments and governors' meetings?

If handled well, this sort of participation allows students to learn how to make their voice heard and to understand how power is deployed. Probably the most important factor is to ensure that the experience for young people is educational and that there is professional collaboration (with appropriate leadership from staff) between teachers and students. Most university students' unions offer guidance for representatives and the issues discussed in this book about school councils are very relevant.

IDEA

71

Working with Governors

Governors are a key part of the school but too often they remain rather shadowy figures who are unknown to the student population. A number of ways can be developed in order to ensure that the governance of the school is clear to the students.

1. A governor could be invited to talk briefly and generally to an assembly about the work of the governing body.
2. An annual or termly meeting could be timetabled between the school council and the governing body.
3. Invitations to events that involve the governors could be extended to members of the school council or other school students.
4. Working groups that are established from the whole governing body could include a school student.
5. A governor could be invited to specific citizenship lessons to discuss issues about how the school is managed.
6. More ambitiously, a form of twinning could go on so that a school student visited another school's governing body and then reported back to the home school governing body on what they were doing.
7. Links can be made between the students, the governors and the person within the local authority who can describe good practice and suggest issues to consider further. As citizenship is often concerned with exploring power, the opportunities that are available locally to understand more about, and to work with, those who are powerful should be taken.
8. Consider showing programmes to students from Teachers' TV that are designed to explain the role of governors. These programmes are normally directed at governors rather than young people, so careful selection and explanation will be needed. But the knowledge that can be derived from such material will help students to ask better questions and to work more effectively with governors.

IDEA 72

Setting Up an Environmental Club

Students are keen to become involved in work that relates to the environment. It is possible to involve students in the consultations established by local councils who undertake ward reviews into how budgets should be allocated. Many councils are very happy to allow teachers to use the same questionnaires that are used in these consultation exercises with adults and to accept the responses the students make.

It is possible for students to suggest environmental projects as they respond to the local city council or to propose something within the school itself, perhaps through the school council. It is not uncommon for schools to establish surveys into matters such as water management in the school with recommendations made and targets set. It might be a good idea to emphasize the key elements of the work through a catchy acronym such as ROAR (research; organise; act; reflect).

These sorts of projects can be very positive if they allow for a review of the activities of those who seem to be powerful as well as merely becoming part of the decision-making process itself. It would be helpful if the work could form part of an annual cycle with decisions made and targets set in the autumn and achievements (or lack of them) reported on by the end of the academic year.

Try to become involved with larger international organisations such as World Wildlife Federation (WWF). Explore the implications of what the students are suggesting and doing. Are they pursuing what is known as an ecocentrist approach or are they more inclined to technocentrism, that is, can technology help us solve our problems or is it the cause of our difficulties? Are they restricting themselves to promoting something like recycling that might implicitly accept, for example, excessive packaging, are they focusing on being a green consumer buying or not buying certain products and/or are they taking a more wide ranging environmental approach that could have political aspects?

SECTION 9

What Can I Do to Set Up and Run a School Council?

IDEA

73

The Purpose of a School Council

School councils can teach students a great deal about the democratic process and encourage them to practise the skills of participation. Schools are not democracies but it's vital to proceed positively and help students to realize that as well as learning how to be a citizen they will have a very good chance of achieving real success along the way.

Lessons could be held within the citizenship programme to inform and discuss with all school students the aims, structures and processes that are relevant to the council. Students will need to be told when and how the elections will be managed, what an agenda looks like, how many meetings will be held each term and so on. A great starter for the class is to discuss what comes into their minds when they hear the term 'school council'? There will be a variety of responses some positive, some negative.

Divide the class into small groups to discuss possible ways of viewing a council. Students could be asked if they agree or disagree with the following and how they could work to ensure that their preferred vision could develop.

1. The council teaches people how to do things such as planning, persuading others, presenting a case, etc. This is a form of political training or education. What skills will the councillors need?
2. A council is a way of allowing young people freedom and responsibility. The essence of this approach is that it helps people to interact with others. The nature of the interaction is personal. It is not important to think about political skills but rather to consider people's ability to get along with others.
3. A council is there to make real improvements in the school. If it fails to make things happen then it is not worth having.

It is possible to develop the above as a staff development exercise. In that context, the links between skills-based teaching, affective goals and education through realistic political activism could be explored in some depth, perhaps emphasizing different approaches to education. Of course, it is also worth explicitly considering what can be done to minimize the negative potential associated with a council that does not work.

KEY TEXT:

Baginsky, M. and Hannam, D. (1999), *School Councils: the views of students and teachers.* London: NSPCC.

School Councils UK (2001), *Secondary Pupil Council DIY Resource Pack*. London: School Councils UK.

And see the Teachers' TV video at www.teachers.tv/videos/speak-out.

IDEA

74

What Can You Do to Help Councillors Form an Agenda for Meetings?

Training sessions with councillors should help them consider the extent of their responsibilities and the limits of what they could achieve. It will serve little purpose if councillors come to a meeting wanting to argue for the abolition of school uniforms if staff are not prepared to begin to consider it.

To what extent will the council agenda follow an issue based format (anyone can suggest anything?) or is there to be a common pattern for each meeting based, for example, around your groups? There should be attention to the development of an agenda that recognizes the following:

1. The use of appropriate forms of communication and discussion to allow for a positive result;
2. The ordering of items so that the one that is regarded as the most desirable by councillors is given an appropriate position (the last agenda item is normally not given as much attention as other items).

One of the simplest ways to help the council achieve status is to make available some small amounts of money that can be spent in line with the wishes of the whole student body and with the final decision of the council.

Councillors have their own constituencies to whom they must report successfully, or, just like a politician who does not deliver, they will lose authority and respect and the whole system will fail. Consultation can take place with the wider student body about the issues they want to see raised; consultation can also occur by councillors or by a teacher on their behalf with members of staff in order to see what issues might be raised. For example:

1. whether money raising activities should take place for particular causes
2. whether a non-school uniform day is to be held

3. whether it is possible to purchase additional facilities in the library or elsewhere in the school
4. how to respond to difficult matters such as bullying or vandalism

IDEA

75

Helping Councillors Prepare for Discussions in Council Meetings

In the following exercise, which is a slightly modified form of a game described by Plous (1993), participants could be asked to realize that at times people find it very difficult to stop and accept other views. At times winning and losing (by saving face or achieving a concrete outcome) may seem to be the most important factor. But councillors need to be reminded that the council can allow for an opportunity for people to learn. They are learning to discuss and discussing to learn.

The game is called 'How much would you pay for £1?' There are five rules:

1. no communication is allowed between the bidders while the auction is underway
2. bids can only be made in multiples of 5p
3. bids must not exceed £5
4. the two highest bidders would both have to pay what they bid even though the £1 only goes to the highest bidder
5. real money is not to be used

There are two crucial points in the game: first, when the two highest bids added together exceed £1 (so, the auctioneer is guaranteed a profit); second, when one of the bids reaches £1. In the first case the bidders will suffer a collective loss and it is interesting to see whether they decide to continue or not. In the second case, it seems odd for a person to continue to bid over £1 even though only £1 can be 'won'. But, if a person feels that they have just lost 95p because their competitor has bid £1, it can appear to be sensible for them to bid just a little more. They may see themselves in competition, not with the auctioneer from whom they can gain £1 but rather, with another bidder. It suddenly becomes possible for them to rationalize the need to bid a lot more than £1 in order to win this new competition.

The above game can be used as an illustration of the way in which those involved in discussion lose sight of what should really matter. It is possible to discuss real situations in which this sort of thing has happened. For example: 'why do people carry on building weapons if they already have enough to destroy the world'?

IDEA 76

Ask students to review the constitution of a school council. This could be from a neighbouring school or their own school. They should be asked to review this material following explanation and discussion about the nature and purpose of a council.

The following questions might help councillors to focus on some challenging issues:

1. do you think that the constitution is sufficiently clear about its purpose?
2. do you think that the constitution distributes power appropriately between staff and pupils?
3. do you think that there should be other matters included in the constitution (e.g. to do with the activities to be undertaken by the council members and the resource available for that work).

The above questions can also be used to review other matters such as peer mentoring schemes.

Following this exercise, students could be asked to undertake a number of tasks:

1. write their own constitution
2. compare the constitution shown below with the arrangements that are in place currently within their school
3. interview two pupils in different year groups and two members of staff (one of whom is a member of the council and one who is not) to ask about the purpose of the council, where the balance of power lies and its effectiveness.

If this work is done well, students will have a better understanding of ideas and issues to do with advocacy, representation, authority, power and legitimation. They will recognize the difficulties for individuals and groups. Not everyone in the school and local community will agree on the ideas being put forward, so there needs to be awareness of what is felt to be right and what is seen as achievable.

There are many simple ways in which councillors can be guided into reporting back effectively For example:

1. Listening to a TV programme and then reporting back the main features. In this way students can practise the skill of remembering and passing on information and ideas.
2. Traditional note taking exercises (for which there are many published guides already available) could help.
3. Reading a newspaper report and then passing on the key points in a limited time will concentrate minds.

Some discussion about voice (tone, volume, etc.) and body language would help. Attention needs to be paid to reporting to different audiences. Some obvious differences between a report made to a group of younger students and then the same issues raised with a group of staff would be the language level used and also the focus on certain aspects of the report that are felt to be of particular interest to the group.

The context of a presentation needs to be considered: talking with an individual requires a certain style; reporting to a year group in an assembly demands a very different approach. Also it would be helpful to discuss the various ways in which messages can become garbled. Inaccuracies can creep into reports. By inclusion or omission, reports can become accidentally biased.

Finally, councillors should be asked to consider the purpose of the feedback. Is the report designed simply to let other people know what happened? Or, is the council or individual councillors trying to persuade people? To emphasize these points about bias it might help, especially with younger groups, to discuss simple optical illusions. Things do not appear the same to all people and councillors need to be aware of different perceptions as they report back.

SECTION 10

What Can I Do to Set Up a Mock Election?

IDEA 78

The Purposes of a Mock Election

There are many purposes to a mock election but some of the most obvious are:

1. to promote understanding of party politics
2. to develop awareness of contemporary issues
3. to provide opportunities for the demonstration and development of the skills of debate and public speaking

You could simply present the positive aspects and goals of a mock election campaign to students, but it may be more helpful through an assembly or lessons to ask students to offer what *they* think are the advantages of a campaign and then to ask them to prioritize these objectives. Then undertake some very basic work on elections in a citizenship lesson:

1. how many people voted in the last general/local/ European elections
2. what sort of people voted (e.g. older people tend to vote more than young people)
3. why might there be concerns about people voting
4. would it be useful to make voting a legal requirement
5. should the age at which people are allowed to vote be reduced to 16
6. should there be fixed terms (in the US there must be a presidential election every 4 years; in this country the government decides when it calls an election within a 5 year period)
7. should we retain the first past the post system or move to a form of proportional representation
8. should we have more elections (e.g. should every city and town have an elected mayor?)

Detailed, but very accessible, data that would help give answers to all the above questions (up to the 2001 result) is available at a number of sites including www.parliament.uk/commons/lib/research/rp2003/rp03–059.

pdf. The Electoral Commission web pages contain useful information and their Do Politics Centre provides valuable resources. The Centre for Research on Elections and Social Trends (CREST) provides some interesting papers (see www.crest.ox.ac.uk/).

IDEA 79

Organizations that Offer Support for Mock Elections

The websites of the Electoral Commission (www.electoralcommission.gov.uk/) and the Hansard Society (in particular the Y vote pages at www.mockelections.co.uk/resources.asp) are very valuable. The pack of resources includes pre-election lessons (which include details about political parties and voting); additional resources (including links to the Democracy Cookbook produced by the Electoral Commission) and post-election lesson which encourages reflection on what went well and what could have been improved. There is, of course, also the pack of materials which helps teachers to organize the mock election itself. There is a good variety of resources including Cd Roms and television programmes and many links to the resources produced by other organizations. In the 2010 mock general election 528 schools took part so this is something that has become part of mainstream educational activity.

It is possible to devise one's own activities but signing up to an established programme has a number of advantages. The materials and activities are, of course, already available and even if they are modified there will be less work needed than if you started from the very beginning. Also, given the potentially controversial nature of elections, it can be useful to have the security of working in ways suggested by respected organizations such as Hansard. The BBC (through Blue Peter and other programmes for children) often support mock elections by providing positive news stories about work being done in schools.

The Federal Trust (www.fedtrust.co.uk) produces materials on European elections. Many US universities (e.g. University of Virginia www.youthleadership.net/index.jsp) produce teaching resources on elections and other matters. Also in the US the Pew Research Centre is a useful source of papers that can help in the creation of teaching resources (see http://people-press.org/).

IDEA 80

What Timetable Should Be Established in Advance of Polling Day?

A 3 week timetable is great as this is the normal length of time between the announcement of the UK general election and polling day. It's essential to plan ahead so that, in advance of the work to be undertaken agreement has been reached with key members of staff. Permission is needed generally to stage the event and more specific details should be agreed about the use of specific spaces in the school (e.g. for posters to be displayed or for meetings to be held). There will also need to be clarity about how students will act (e.g. will the head teacher be comfortable with candidates talking to the local media?) Agreement needs to be reached about which students are to be involved – does everyone have a vote in one election or are there different elections for different parts of the school? It is very important to prepare in advance for the evaluation of the election.

Decisions will need to be taken well in advance about whether to allow students to use their own party labels or to insist on the use of the largest and mainstream political parties. There is a potential problem if students were to decide to stand for a legal political party such as the British National Party or, less controversially, create a joke party. An easy way to avoid such problems would be to make clear from the outset that only mainstream parties would be allowed. When I managed mock elections in schools I did not impose this sort of restriction in advance (but I suspect that I would not have allowed a group to stand that would threaten the security of other pupils or to denigrate the whole process).

The following jobs/issues need to be allocated and worked out at an early stage:

1. briefings to staff
2. choose individual members of staff to liaise with specific groups
3. arrange for ballot papers to be printed (including arrangements over postal votes)

4. arrange for staff to manage hustings, count votes and interpret results
5. announce the election to students and invite nominations
6. ensure students are involved with staff in the jobs mentioned above (e.g. counting votes and interpreting results)

It is possible to use different frameworks but the following is one that I have seen work reasonably well:

Students arrive at school and go to an assembly (year assemblies work best if one has devised constituencies based on age groups or allowed for party machines that include several candidates) in which there is an opportunity for final speeches made by candidates. The students may then go to a brief session with their tutor in which ballot papers are distributed and a ballot box is available. This approach virtually guarantees a very high turnout. If this is felt to be unhelpfully unrealistic it would be possible for ballot boxes to be set up in different locations around the school during morning break and lunchtime. If this latter approach is followed, care would need to be exercised to ensure that specific groups were directed to particular polling stations and that there was identification checks.

The end of lunchtime should be the latest time allowed for voting to occur, thus the early part of the afternoon is made available for counting of the ballots. The count can be undertaken by staff and students who have been appointed in advance and who are seen as being impartial. The results can be announced using the system agreed in advance (probably first past the post).

During the next few days a series of interviews can be held with candidates during assemblies or published on the school intranet and analyses of the results can be undertaken to use different systems (e.g. proportional representation) and to raise issues about the level of involvement of different groups. It will be very useful to compare the school results with what actually happened in the real general election. In the 2010 'Y vote' the Liberal Democrats achieved a massive victory.

IDEA 82

Evaluating the Event?

There are three key ways in which the event can be analyzed:

1. Rather intangible factors should be explored. What was the atmosphere like during the election? Was there a positive sense of involvement, with teachers and students engaged in lively and constructive democratic debate? This can be done through discussion in form groups and also by the use of questionnaires.
2. Simple counting should be undertaken in order to establish the level of involvement. How many posters were displayed? How many people attended hustings? How many and what types of students voted? If this is to be done successfully the evaluation plans need to be agreed in advance.
3. Educational issues should be probed. What sort of knowledge and skills are revealed? Were speeches of high quality? Were questions asked that were focused and based on good understanding? Did the posters reflect key issues with appropriate language being used? In this context you are more of an assessor using skills used by English teachers (language), history teachers (political concepts), mathematics teachers (understanding of economic indicators), science teachers (appreciation of the significance of environmental matters, etc.). Again, it would be useful to include students in this work.

The above three considerations should be analyzed by a team of students and teachers. They could take the role of election observers (as occurs in major national elections around the world). It would be interesting to involve others in this process including governors or, more ambitiously, people from outside the school perhaps from political parties or community groups.

It will be very important to provide a platform for the delivery of these results. Proper reflection on what happened will provide a good way of building confidence, developing knowledge and skills and helping to provide a solid basis for the next mock election.

SECTION 11

Citizenship Lessons

IDEA

83

'Anything Can Happen in the Next Few Days . . .'

There used to be a children's TV series in which at moments of crisis someone in a rather frantic manner would claim that 'anything can happen in the next half hour'! You can use this 'hook' to generate some interest in contemporary news stories and make the very important point that we are always unsure how things will develop.

Choose a recent newspaper story that deals with a crisis. Describe very briefly the background to the story and then present the class with three alternative outcomes. Two of these should be fairly simple and straightforward and one should allow for a slightly fuller and perhaps more subtle response.

For example, if a politician had been accused of negligence or abuse of office, a story might appear suggesting that he or she should be terminated. Following a brief summary of the key issues in the story the class could be given the options:

1. yes, he or she will be sacked (or made to resign)
2. he or she will continue to do the job
3. something else . . . please explain

It is important to develop a lively atmosphere and perhaps, on occasion, to generate a bit of fun as students make their decision. But it is ESSENTIAL, of course, that stories are treated appropriately. A game show atmosphere should not be allowed to develop over serious matters to do with personal and public tragedies. Keep a record of the final outcome and tell the class as soon as possible what actually happened (try to pick issues that will be resolved quickly).

Some students may complain that they cannot be involved, as their views would never be taken into account while these decisions were made. So, remind them that public opinion does matter and we all play a part in that (however small).

This exercise could lead with some to a discussion about the nature of our formal democratic system that is largely based on representative rather than participatory processes.

IDEA 84

What's the Story?

This is a version of Pictionary and students will respond easily and positively to the exercise. Divide the class into two teams.

Each side is asked in turn to draw something that illustrates a person or story from public life or a feature of our democracy. The list of people or topics to be guessed by the class is developed by you beforehand and passed to the student who will draw. The other members of the team on the same side as the person who is drawing the picture are asked to guess what story is being referred to. If they guess correctly they are awarded two points. If they fail to guess then the other side have a chance to gain one point.

The first team to receive at least five points is the winner. You can provide a little explanation for each of the drawings once the points have been awarded. The value of this for citizenship depends on the items that are chosen to be drawn and the quality of the brief explanations given by the students and/or you. It is important that it is not seen as a party game. It should link to the work being done by the class and thus will focus on political concepts, skills, contexts, etc. The items could be selected in order to provide brief explanations about:

1. formal politics (Houses of Parliament; the Queen; European Union flag; symbol of the United Nations)
2. contemporary stories (price of oil goes up/down; war; pensions crisis; changes in the health service)
3. individuals (scope for all those budding cartoonists who can caricature or accurately represent leading figures.

IDEA

85

Odd One Out!

Odd one out exercises are now very common in many classrooms. Provide a list of four words and ask pupils to choose the odd one out and then give their reasons for their decision. Some examples of lists are given below (of course, in some cases the names would have to be changed to ensure that the activity was up to date and that students would know something about the items):

1. David Cameron; Nick Clegg; the Queen; Vince Cable (odd one out is the Queen as all others are members of the coalition government established in 2010).
2. Shopping; voting; playing; travelling (voting is the odd one out as the other activities can be done by people younger than 18).
3. Local council; European parliament; House of Commons; Greenpeace (Greenpeace is the odd one out as it is a pressure group).
4. France; Greece; Germany; Switzerland (Switzerland is the odd one out as it is not a member of the European Union).

This exercise could be expanded into a full lesson if a long list of items was given with students being asked to group them into categories. There will in most cases be a right answer and the exercise can be used simply to reinforce factual knowledge. But often it will be possible to have a range of appropriate responses. The key will be to ensure that the exercise is used as a stimulating platform for explanation and further discussion.

Students could investigate a particular election from the past or be asked to predict how an election that is about to happen will develop.

The 2000 US election may now be too dated for many students in schools to feel a strong connection but there is a fascinating story to be investigated about:

1. The share of the popular vote.
2. The crucial position of Florida (whose governor at the time, Jeb Bush, is the brother of the eventual winner, George Bush).
3. The debates about voting papers that had been designed to be read by computers (people had often not completely cut through the part of the slip known as a chad to show their preferences so a bizarre sequence of events occurred in which judgments had to be made about the meaning of a 'dimpled chad', 'hanging chad' and so on).
4. Who was called in to make the final decision about who won (the position of the individuals on the Supreme Court is very interesting).

Perhaps the more up to date 2010 British election would be a case study that appeals more easily to students. The result meant that no clear party achieved an overall majority. So, how could a government be formed? Students could be presented with the result and asked to suggest ways forward. If two parties combine would that be a good way forward, or would that mean that people had been tricked? No one voted directly for a coalition so why should that be the form of government that is established? Or, should we see this as a great opportunity to move beyond negative politics to something that is more co-operative? Then more detail could be done on the policies to be followed by the new government. With younger students a few examples of policies could be shown in order to allow suggestions to be made about what should be done. With older students the Conservative and Liberal Democrat manifestoes could be presented and they could be asked to come up with their own suggestions for the policies of the coalition.

IDEA 87

How Do You Feel About That?

Introduce the class to an issue, a trend or a story. The material could be drawn from any aspect of the citizenship syllabus. For example:

1. the number of people who voted in the last election
2. the price of houses
3. the rate of inflation
4. the prospects for war in a particular part of the world

Distribute (or just show on the board) a set of faces showing different expressions (happy, sad, confused, frightened). Ask the students to make clear their feelings about a particular issue by selecting one of the faces. They can select a face by drawing it in their exercise book or by a show of hands as the teacher points to each picture that has been displayed on the board. Then ask why they feel that way and what (if anything) they can do about it and will do about it.

With some classes, it will be enough to show three fairly obvious emotions by using simple drawings of faces (happy, sad, angry) but of course depending on the ability of the class and your skills as an artist the sky is the limit! With older and more able students it is possible to probe more fully into why they feel certain things. Some students will be able to deal with fairly subtle distinctions. Are they identifying something that is:

1. serious and/or problematic
2. important now and/or in relation to a trend
3. important in absolute terms and/or relative to other things
4. important for all and/or a particular segment of society

A great deal of work can be done on the ways in which politicians use language. Students might enjoy the possibilities of exploring a few of the well-known sayings of politicians. They could read the following and then be asked to choose their favourite and explain why they find it attractive (or, explain why they feel it would not work):

1. *Ask not what your country can do for you but what you can do for your country* (John F. Kennedy).
2. *Tough on crime and tough on the causes of crime* (Tony Blair).
3. *Where there is discord may we bring harmony.*
4. *Where there is error may we bring truth.*
5. *Where there is doubt may we bring faith.*
6. *Where there is despair, may we bring hope* (Margaret Thatcher after St. Francis of Assisi).
7. *Never in the field of human conflict has so much been owed by so many to so few.* (Winston Churchill).
8. *I may have the body of a weak and feeble woman but I have the heart and stomach of a king.* (Elizabeth I)

Students may be interested to see how often a word or phrase is used three times (look at the above example in the quotation by Churchill when 'so' is used three times or, from another quotation, think about Blair's 'education, education, education'). Look also for sharp contrasts (the quotation from Thatcher is a whole series of contrasting opposites). A development of the use of contrast can be seen in what I tend to think of as 'turning the phrase' (the examples from Kennedy and Blair shown above illustrate the way a reordering of the sentence gives the listener a puzzle to work out as well as a contrast to learn).

There is a whole series of lessons that could be based around citizenship and literacy or citizenship and media studies. There is a whole scheme of work that could be done about 'spin doctors'.

KEY TEXT:

Beard, A. (2000), *The Language of Politics*. London: Routledge.

IDEA

89

The Post-it Plenary

The highlighting of key objectives throughout the lesson is now an established part of a teacher's repertoire and the use of Post-it notes to emphasize specific points is widespread.

In a citizenship lesson you may have asked the students to think about freedoms in society today and have involved the class in a series of activities which allowed them to consider 'freedom from' and 'freedom to'. Students could have examined different groups or individuals in society who want different things. One group could want the freedom to do certain things but another group could object by claiming that they want the freedom from being dominated by their opponents.

There are many simple or complex ideas that can emerge from such a lesson (or series of lessons). At the end of a lesson you might want to know more about the reaction of the class and could simply ask them to put their Post-it notes on a board. They could ask questions, refer to additional contexts that had not been mentioned in the lesson or give their own views about which of the opposing groups they feel to be in the right. Some classes will need guidance about how to respond in ways that are appropriately constructive.

This could provide useful material for an end of lesson discussion or show you what needs to be clarified. A more structured approach would be for you to ask 'what have you learned in this lesson' and insist that all students reply (giving a named slip of paper to you as the leave the room would allow for a reasonably high chance of a considered esponse). Or, you could remind students of the learning objectives for the lesson and ask for students to give a mark out of ten to show how confident they now feel about understanding that objective.

IDEA 90

The Answer Depends on the Question

One way to generate students' understanding of opinion poll data is to allow them to devise a questionnaire of their own. As a full-fledged exercise, this could take a considerable amount of time (easily six or seven lessons could be covered by discussing the use of opinion polls, the ways in which questions can be devised and how the results can be analyzed).

I think an excellent lesson can be devised solely around the question of what does it mean if I've just told an opinion pollster 'I don't know'. Very good ideas can be developed about 'don't know' meaning a lack of knowledge or a refusal to co-operate or a high level of awareness that has led to a difficulty in making a decision about a controversial issue. It is possible to give some very quick activities about questions and how they can be used. One brief activity is to provide a list of flawed questions and then ask students to spot the errors.

How popular is the prime minister?

The first 200 people met in the central shopping centre on Friday morning will be asked. All those people will answer all the questions shown below.

a) How old are you? Circle one of the categories shown below:
   15–25; 25–35; 35–55; 55–75
b) Do you think that the prime minister is doing a better job than the previous prime minister or do you think he could do a bit better? Circle one of the categories shown below:
   yes; no; don't know
c) The prime minister is clearly an intelligent person and most are happy with his performance? Do you agree? Circle one of the categories shown below:
   yes; no; don't know
d) Do you not think that the prime minister should spend a little more money on hospitals?
   yes; no; don't know

e) Given that the money supply in the UK is subject to a range of factors associated with exogenous growth how do you think the prime minister should deal with inflation?

. . . .

Of course, all the questions shown above are hopeless. The first 200 people met in a shopping centre on a Friday morning would not give a representative group. It would be unwise to insist that all questions must be answered (although one can do one's best to achieve a full response). The first question gives overlapping age boundaries and excludes those who are younger than 15 or older than 75 (it is acceptable to deliberately exclude certain people for specific reasons but there is no justification for this given here). The second question asks for more than one response but only allows one simple answer. The third question is a leading question.

The fourth question is very difficult to answer (and the answers would be very difficult to interpret) as it is given in the form of a negative question. People in some parts of the UK use the negative interrogative frequently in their speech and so care would be needed if the questionnaire is to be read to respondents (students will not always read what is on the page). The last question is full of jargon that will simply confuse respondents.

Many other types of weak question could be developed for students to spot examples of bad practice (e.g. assuming that the respondent will agree with a particular opinion as they belong to a specific group – such as assuming that all older people will agree with pension increases).

Students could carry out a case study of the involvement of a controversial figure in a TV programme. The episode of Question Time which featured Nick Griffin of the British National Party (BNP) would perhaps be one example of what could be useful.

It is important to emphasise that this sort of controversial matter would be appropriate only in certain circumstances. It is the responsibility of the teacher to judge the general context in the community, the school and what individual students can cope with.

1. Students should be provided with, or research themselves, in order to understand the context. The position of the BNP as a legal political party, its electoral support (in local and national elections) and its policies. The nature of Nick Griffin – what he has said and what he has been involved with in the past. The role of the BBC as a broadcaster charged with the responsibility of ensuring that the public is provided with information and with discussions of key issues. The more particular criteria that Question Time has for inviting guests onto the programme (a certain amount of electoral support triggers the possibility of inclusion);
2. The programme itself could be watched. (Various segments of the broadcast appear on Youtube). What was asked and how did the panel respond to the audience and to each other? What do students think was the overall effect on the standing of Nick Griffin?
3. Students should investigate the comments made about the programme after the broadcast. What seems to have been the general reaction? Did it seem that the public were convinced by Griffin or was opposition to him strengthened? What was Griffin's reaction? Most important, what was the reaction from within the BNP to Griffin? Is it possible that the organization was weakened?

Wider questions could be raised as a result of this case study:

1. to what extent should we allow free speech
2. should we decide to allow certain views to be expressed as long as they supported by a sufficiently large number of people
3. who has the responsibility to stand up for a decent society
4. how do we decide the meaning of decency

The (Dis)united Kingdom?

The United Kingdom comprises England, Scotland, Wales and Northern Ireland. Colley (1992) has traced the historical development of the UK suggesting that the nation was 'forged' on the anvil of wars (most of which were won by England) and perhaps asks us to think whether we have been left with something that is coherent or a 'forgery'.

Today, the Houses of Parliament are located in London in England and there is a Scottish Parliament, a Welsh Assembly and a Northern Ireland Assembly. There are general issues that can be investigated about the appropriateness of these general arrangements. There are issues about what counts as nation(s) and the political structure(s) that should be applied to them. (Cornwall would, at one time, have been regarded as something like a nation).

The Scottish Parliament opened in 1999. Elections are held every 4 years. Every person has eight MSPs who work for them (one in the local constituency and the others located in different areas). The Parliament can make laws about what are called devolved matters – transport, health, housing, education, sport, Gaelic, farming, etc. Reserved matters are those that the Parliament cannot make laws about and include taxes, benefits, defence, gambling, etc. As a result of the 2007 election the Scottish National Party forms the government and their leader is known as First Minister.

Issues to discuss:

1. Do these arrangements mean that it is more or less likely that in the future the UK will still exist;
2. What should be done to resolve disagreements between the UK parliament and the Scottish Parliament;
3. Will different systems mean that people are likely to move to or away from certain areas (e.g. Scottish university students pay a much smaller fee than those who live in England;

4. Generally, what do students think about the 'Midlothian question': is it fair that MPs from Scotland at the Westminster may decide about things that apply in England but English MPs are not members of the Scottish Parliament?

KEY TEXT:

Colley, L. (1992), *Britons 1707–1837: forging the nation.* New York and London: Yale University Press.

Citizenship in democratic, pluralistic and decent societies is always concerned with trying to do the right thing. But there are, of course, always terribly difficult decisions to take. Examine the following case study and see what students feel about the rights of individuals and how decisions can be taken:

Sue and Harriet were conjoined twins. Sue was weaker and was literally drawing life (in the form of blood supply) away from her sister. If the twins were not separated then both would die. If they were separated then Sue would definitely die but her sister would have the chance to survive. The parents were deeply religious and felt that the terrible dilemma that they were facing was perhaps only capable of being resolved by letting nature take its course. The case came to court and the judges eventually decided that separation should occur. Sue died. Harriet survived.

There is an awful tragedy here and it is vital to proceed with huge sensitivity. Real people's lives are to be respected. There are, however, important issues about rights and responsibilities and this is what citizenship is about. Perhaps one way of dealing with these matters would be to address some of the issues through fictional situations which are believable and have elements that relate to such personal tragedies. The novels of Jodi Picoult are often read by young people. They often focus on a moral dilemma. Reading a novel is not enough in itself for a citizenship lesson. A professional educator has to take that material, identify its learning potential and to develop a strategy for action. A citizenship concept (e.g. rights) should be selected, there needs to be content which is appropriate for the age group and ability of the class, there should be opportunities to learn about participation and there needs to be a sensible approach to assessment. I am not suggesting that there should be a test on the right answer; there needs to be improved understanding.

IDEA

94

Tackling Controversy

The Crick report included an appendix on the teaching of controversial issues. Teachers must be aware of what can and should be done as we tackle controversy. The following guidelines will be useful:

1. Decide what controversy means. Is it about the importance of the issue itself (e.g. abortion is controversial – football is not?); the number of people who are involved (only a few people arguing for something mean that it is not controversial because it does not lead to anything happening?).
2. When does controversy become problematic? In many lessons there is an element of controversy. When an investigation is academic (e.g. 'is Hamlet mad') there are usually no problems for teachers. When an issue is about values teachers need to tread carefully. Also teachers need to be careful when it appears that something is being proposed rather than just discussed.
3. Local factors are important. A debate about the disposal of nuclear waste is 'interesting' in one area of the UK and potentially upsetting and explosive in another area.
4. What teaching methods should be employed? Are students used to discussing issues in other parts of the school? Are they old enough and mature enough to handle the particular controversy? Is there factual information which can help students to understand the key issue? Is the teacher to be a neutral chair? Should a teacher play devil's advocate?

My answers to these questions are that a controversial issue in one over which society is divided and usually relates to morality. Issues are more or less controversial depending on circumstances (local factors and the nature of the learners). Teachers will use a variety of teaching approaches but will normally dip in and out of all those mentioned above (neutral, advocate, devil's advocate). In other words, a proper understanding of the general nature of controversy and close attention to local factors will help a teacher to develop an appropriate response. Context is vital: general guidelines can only go so far.

KEY TEXT:

The appendix to the Crick report written by Alex Porter. (see www.teachingcitizenship.org.uk/dnloads/crickreport1998.pdf).

IDEA

95

Every Picture Tells a Story

Cartoons are full of symbols and the best ones can make people laugh and tell people about an issue while making them think more deeply about the underlying political and economic factors in society. But cartoons can also be very difficult for young people to understand especially if they are not very familiar with contemporary news stories.

You can use pictures in a variety of easier ways. For example, show students a photo from a newspaper. Small groups could be asked to come to the front of the class, memorise the key features and return to their desks. Give them 30 seconds to write down the main features of the picture and then discuss what they have written (simple description) and then what they think the picture shows (an opportunity for a more analytical response).

Alternatively, each student could be given a photocopy of a picture from a newspaper and asked to label the key features. Again a discussion could then take place about what the picture was showing. At times this sort of approach can be used simply to get across the story itself but it can also be used to show how a picture has been taken in a certain way to contribute to a particular version of events (does a picture of a politician crying arouse our sympathy?; does a picture of a demonstration 'prove' that some people are guilty of violence?)

Another approach is to give different groups of students different pictures. A theme could be chosen to illustrate a theme. For example:

1. is the environment in danger
2. was 2010 a good year
3. is the economy in good shape
4. are all countries in Africa poverty stricken

Each group describes their own picture and by doing so makes clear what story is being told. One member of each small group is then sent to the other groups to find out what other stories are being told by their pictures.

One member of each group remains at 'home' to show the picture to the 'visitors'. The group members return to base and they decide on a final version. The different outcomes are discussed by the whole class.

IDEA

96

What Should We Do?

The local council has decided that the local leisure centre and theatre will be developed. The swimming pool is expensive to maintain and not very well used. There are two other theatres in the small town and there have been increasing problems with attracting famous stars who can pull in the crowds. Large amounts of council tax are being spent on maintaining what it seems is no longer needed.

A successful company, Lively Leisure Ltd., (LLL) has offered a way forward. It wants to build a casino and luxury hotel on the site. Immediately, local residents complain. They like the idea of a leisure centre. It is good for people's health and they say that the alternative will lead only to large profits for the company, heavy drinking and noise especially at the weekends.

Ask the students to form different groups comprising councillors, residents, representative of LLL and observers in order to prepare for a debate. Councillors, residents and the people from LLL each (separately as a group) prepare a statement. The statements from each of the groups will make clear what they want to happen and why.

While these statements are being prepared, tell the group of observers that they will focus on two things during the debate: what is being said and how effectively the points are being made. Discuss with the observers how to listen carefully and what sorts of things to make a note of. The students form small groups of four in which there is one representative from each of the following: the council, LLL and local residents. Each person in this group of four has one minute to speak. When a statement has been made, there is an opportunity for the group to ask questions.

When all statements have been made there is an opportunity for a discussion within the small group. Throughout, the observer in each group makes notes on what is happening. Without using names, the observers provide feedback to the whole class to let others know what points were made and how well they were made.

As the formal statements from the councillors, residents and LLL are the same in each small group, the observers are not expected to report back on that statement although this might be included in a whole class discussion led by you. At the end of the lesson you could draw the threads together about the ways to debate effectively.

IDEA 97

Show Us What You've Got!

Getting students involved in displays is always fun. This could be as simple as displaying their work (posters or video presentations) or asking them to respond to issues in simple ways by having 'true' and 'false' cards which could be raised at specific points in the lesson to show what they think.

Students could be issued with artefacts that relate to a citizenship issue. For a lesson on the environment the following could be used:

1. packaging
2. a leaflet from a pressure group
3. a photo of a factory polluting the atmosphere
4. a supermarket containing goods brought from overseas countries
5. a car
6. people going on holiday by aeroplane.

Organize a 'display exchange' in which the students tell each other what they have. A record is made of what is being shown and then you can discuss what the class has found out.

A slightly different approach is to ask students to find something being held by another student that complements their artefact and be ready to explain why they have chosen that link.

Another way of thinking about display could include the well-known technique of hot seating. In this activity one student is asked (after everyone has had an opportunity to prepare) to play a certain role. The President of the US, for example, could be put on the spot by students asking about the decisions that led to a certain outcome but the roles could be much more down to earth and, with care, include local illustrations.

We get to know about citizenship principally through the media and as such students need to think about how it operates. Try the following:

1. Bring a few national newspapers into a class. Analyze readership figures and target audience (a good summary is available on Wikipedia). Review the reading age necessary for different newspapers (various ways of doing this can be seen at www.cimt.plymouth.ac.uk/resources/topical/reading/reading.htm). Ask students to think about the nature of the media and what that means for the promotion of certain forms of citizenship;
2. Choose three pictures from a newspaper and remove the captions. Pictures of individuals work well but it is also possible to include images of wider contexts. Invite the students to supply their own captions. A photo of a politician looking serious will lead some students to describe a defeat – 'Cameron – weary and worried'. But it is equally possible for a much more positive interpretation to be given of the same image: 'David Cameron carefully considers the best way forward'. The phrasing of these captions can be analyzed – the use of the first or full name; the effect of alliteration (which tends to slow the pace of the reader and gives time for a particular interpretation to be accepted); the implied reference to the past and present in the first caption (a problem has occurred because of what has already happened) and the explicit reference to the future in the second. Students can then be shown the caption that was actually used. On certain occasions different newspapers use the same pictures but with different captions;
3. There are good schemes that are commercially available to help students replicate decision making in the production of a TV news programme. It is fairly straightforward to do something similar yourself. Watch one, 10-minute news broadcast and list the topics and the amount of time taken for each item.

Then ask students to come up with their own running order and time allocations, compare with the original and discuss. What was selected by the broadcaster and by the students as being important and why?

Citizenship education deals with contemporary society and we are regularly asked to believe that the world is facing insurmountable problems. Many examples of this can be developed. But how much of a crisis are we really facing? Is crisis normal? Are crises exploited by people who are manoeuvring for position?

Try the following case study:

Oil spill in the Gulf of Mexico 2010

A well ruptured on 20 April 2010. On 1 June 2010 BP issued a statement which included the comment that:

> 'Over 1,600 vessels are now involved in the response effort, including skimmers, tugs, barges and recovery vessels. Operations to skim oil from the surface of the water have now recovered, in total, some 321,000 barrels (13.5 million gallons) of oily liquid. The total length of containment boom deployed as part of efforts to prevent oil reaching the coast is now over 1.9 million feet, and an additional 1.8 million feet of sorbent boom has also been deployed'.

Tony Hayward, BP's Chief Executive, resigned following criticism.

On 19 September the well was closed and the Guardian reported:

> President Barack Obama, whose approval ratings were hurt by public discontent over the government's initial response to the spill, welcomed an 'important milestone'. Obama said his administration was now focused on making sure the Gulf coast 'recovers fully from this disaster. This road will not be easy, but we will continue to work closely with the people of the Gulf to rebuild their livelihoods and restore the environment that supports them'.

This was clearly a terrible disaster for the environment, for the local people, for BP and for the President of the United States.

Ask students to analyze what was done, and why, by three key actors:

1. Barack Obama
2. Tony Hayward
3. The media

Identify: who was to blame for the spillage; how did they react under pressure; what did they seek to do during the crisis; who, if anyone emerged, with credit from the disaster.

SECTION 12

What Can I Do to Assess Students?

IDEA

100

Introduction to Assessment

Assessment is perhaps one of the most challenging issues for those who are concerned with citizenship education. Some have argued that citizenship education is not something that can be assessed. It is hard to know whether to emphasize knowledge, skills or attitudes and what sort of blend of these areas is possible. It is important to get over these hurdles: we are not assessing citizens; we are assessing students' abilities in citizenship education; we need to clarify the blend of knowledge, understanding, skills and dispositions that we require if students are to demonstrate that they are making progress.

It is now well established that assessment is not just about formal testing and that it does not occur only at the end of a sequence of lessons. Assessment happens all the time (by students as well as teachers) and it is part of good teaching. This commitment to assessment *for* learning (and not just assessment *of* learning) is very valuable.

There are many general resources. The 'planning and assessment in citizenship' pages that are currently housed on the QCDA site are very useful for outlining in broad terms what is required. There are some useful discussion papers about the nature of assessment in citizenship of which one of the best is by Lee Jerome *Planning Assessment for Citizenship Education* (see the citizED site at www.citized.info) More precise information and guidance about assessing particular pieces of students' work is available (e.g. see http://curriculum.qcda.gov.uk/key-stages-3-and-4/assessment/exemplification/standards-files/citizenship/citizenship-level3.aspx). Students' work, with commentaries by assessors, can be seen at the official National Curriculum sites.

It is quite proper as part of our broad roles as teachers to concern ourselves with questions about the extent to which young people are becoming citizens, but I think we need to focus principally on how much students are learning about citizenship and how well they are able to show the skills required to get things done both alone and in the ways they work effectively and responsibly with others.

KEY TEXT:

Black, P. et al. (2003), *Assessment for Learning: Putting it into practice.* Maidenhead, Berkshire: Open University Press.

Kerr, D., Keating, A., and Ireland, E. (2009), *Pupil assessment in citizenship education: purposes, practices and possibilities.* Slough, Berkshire: NFER (see www.nfer.ac.uk/research/projects/cels/)

Of course many will not be comfortable with the idea of using levels, arguing that citizenship does not lend itself to this sort of approach. Levels, of course, may be used for many different purposes. I am not sure that applying them only for the purposes of grading would help.

We need to be careful that citizenship education is not reduced to a series of simple tests. Rather, it might be useful to be clear to oneself and one's students about what is to be regarded as an initial characterization of good practice. There are, broadly, three frameworks against which work can be judged:

1. Norm referencing in which individuals are judged against each other. This is a very traditional method of assessment. It can involve a rigid application of a normal distribution curve (the top 20 per cent for example, will pass whatever standard they have achieved).
2. Criteria referencing, which means that as long as a student demonstrates achievement he or she will pass. This may mean that all may achieve top marks.
3. Ipsative referencing which compares a student against his or her own performance.

In practice norm, criteria and ipsative referencing are used simultaneously. We cannot understand what the standards mean unless they are exemplified and we analyze them by reference to many other things. But, broadly, we now have a much better sense of the criteria for achievement, tell students in advance by referring to levels of response and judge their achievement.

This does not mean that the levels of response for a specific exercise cannot be altered in light of the work that is done by students. Perhaps students will come up with other and better responses than you had imagined. It may also be the case that the level of generality suggested by National Curriculum levels is not appropriate for specific cases.

Assessing understanding in relation to complex and sensitive matters is a key challenge for citizenship teachers. A general framework for thinking about students' ability to explain might include:

1. Pupils are simply confused by a series of events.
2. Pupils explain matters in terms of people being right or wrong. Or at times the actors are seen as being simply unintelligent or intelligent. Often those who lose are seen as being wrong and unskilled. Pupils may at this level make simple, and at times inappropriate, connections. One factor (or a list of separate factors) will explain what happened. There is a description (of, for example, a legal process) rather than analysis. Things happen because people intend them to happen. There is no real attempt to show how factors and individuals interact.
3. Pupils make deliberate efforts to consider both a range of factors and the way in which they interlock. They consider causation and motivation. They look for the relationship between intention and outcome. They view a range of perspectives. They see that narrative order is important is explaining an event. They consider the nature of the relationship between intention and outcome. They are able to comment upon the meaning of relevant value statements.

Lee Jerome has written about work on identity and diversity which asks students to consider why attempts to establish an eruv in a mixed area might be controversial. (An eruv is a boundary established by Jewish law within which certain activities can take place on holy days). He refers to broad levels of response:

1. No understanding of social diversity, only individual difference;
2. Seeing others as foreign and removed from contemporary culture;
3. Confusion about specific groups but no overt hostility;

4. Beginning to understand that differences are linked to groups, context and ways of seeing the world;
5. Beginning to understand that people are shaped by and in turn have agency in interpreting and shaping the idea of the groups to which they belong. Beginning to adopt a more principled accommodation of difference.

We should not be too wary of assessing or evaluating students' involvement in citizenship issues. There is a wealth of experience that can be drawn from contexts such as drama education and a rich variety of vocational education. There are increasing numbers of examples of active citizenship assessments readily available (e.g. www.qcda.gov.uk/resources/522.aspx). Students at Cedar Mount High produced a DVD based on a project about alcohol and drug awareness in an inner city primary school. It was not principally a media project but focused directly on citizenship including rights and responsibilities, enquiry, advocacy and reflection.

There is currently a hopeful but very challenging sense in which we are dealing with new ground. As a very tentative beginning I would like to suggest that the following might not be seen as simple levels but rather that there are areas that might suggest ways to explore matters further.

1. Active thinking/Physical activity: have the students achieved a critical engagement that necessarily involves, practically and academically, doing something?
2. Individually generated activity/Working with, or in relation to, others: can they show individual initiative? Can they work with others?
3. Participation in school/Participation in other contexts: have the school students been offered opportunities to take part in a variety of contexts?
4. Participating/Engaging: are they just taking part or are they really engaged?

We can use a variety of data in considering whether students are achieving success. There will be certain obvious signs of involvement (they perhaps participate in the school council, or we can note the number of contributions they make to discussions for example) and there will also be ways in which we could use evaluation rather than assessment data (i.e. we can ask them if they felt engaged or were just taking part in the way that they had been directed).

IDEA

104

Reporting on Work Done in Citizenship

Reporting in an old-fashioned sense of writing only a summative account of a student's work would not be appropriate for citizenship education. Rather, as well as allowing for the detailed guidance that only the expert teacher can provide, there should be a genuine attempt to recognize the processes implied by the climate that is suitable for citizenship education. I suggest that this means insistence on the good practice already adopted by other subjects.

First, there should be clarity about what is being assessed. Students should understand the nature of the task, its purpose and the possibilities for initiative on their part to transform it, but also the need for them to be clear about the meaning of the numbering or grading system (should one be used). Second, the report should make it clear the nature of what sort of action could or should be taken by a student who wishes to improve in particular areas. In this sense, all reports are formative.

Third, there should be, through a variety of processes, involvement by the student in the generation of a judgement. At times this will mean the completion by a student of a stand-alone self-assessment tool that has only informal status. At others, there may be room for decisions to be negotiated between teacher and student. It may be possible for the students to write their own self-assessments (although of course this would need to be discussed with a teacher).

Reporting should occur in a range of different ways. Oral as well as written feedback is useful. Fixed and formal reporting points should be supplemented by informal, frequent feedback. There should be a variety of audiences (carers, students, other teachers, etc.)

Three points are vital: the report should focus on understanding and skills that are an essential part of citizenship education; it should be positive and valuable to the learner and others; and, it should be done in ways that are manageable (teachers writing hundreds of lengthy reports are not always making the best use of their time).

SECTION

13

Examinations

IDEA

105

GCSE Citizenship Studies

GCSE is an excellent way to raise the status of citizenship education in the school. There has been some debate about the use of the word 'studies' (reflecting the concern of some that there is an insufficient focus on action) but my personal view is that it is possible to do excellent work through these programmes. It provides motivation, focus and tangible achievement. The number of candidates has been increasing, it is now possible to take a full, as well as a short, course and there are good resources available.

All GCSE courses have to meet certain specifications (details on the Ofqual site www.ofqual.gov.uk/files/qca-07–3443_gcsecriteriacitizenship.pdf). Generally, those in citizenship should encourage learners to be inspired, moved and changed by following a broad, coherent, satisfying and worthwhile course of study. This should enable learners to gain the confidence and conviction to participate in decision making and play an active role as effective citizens in public life.

More precisely, the course must enable learners to:

1. Engage with topical citizenship issues and contribute to debates on challenges facing society involving a wide range of political, social and ethical ideas, issues and problems in different contexts (local to global).
2. Develop and apply understanding of key citizenship concepts (justice, democracy, rights and responsibilities, identities and diversity) to deepen their understanding of society and how communities change over time.
3. Use an enquiring, critical approach to distinguish facts, opinions and bias, build arguments and make informed judgments.
4. Develop the necessary skills, knowledge and understanding to take action with others to address citizenship issues in their communities.

There is a reasonable degree of flexibility about the content of the GCSE programme. The content must,

view of interview data); what sections do I expect
y report to have (and, later in the exercise, what
gument am I making?).

content and focus of projects can vary from those
investigate transport issues using the perspectives
cal residents, to international enquiries gathering
from school students in other parts of the country
orld, to practical engagement that aims to achieve
ecific outcome.

of course, reflect the learning outcomes and must be consistent with the National Curriculum.

There are three assessment objectives:

AO1 Recall, select and communicate their knowledge and understanding of citizenship concepts, issues and terminology (assessment weighting: 25–35 per cent).

AO2 Apply skills, knowledge and understanding when planning, taking and evaluating citizenship actions in a variety of contexts (assessment weighting: 40–50 per cent).

AO3 Analyze and evaluate issues and evidence including different viewpoints to construct reasoned arguments and draw conclusions (assessment weighting: 30–40 per cent).

GCSE specifications in citizenship studies must allocate a weighting of 40 per cent to external assessment and a weighting of 60 per cent to controlled assessment in the overall scheme of assessment.

IDEA 106

What is Offered by the Three Examination Boards?

All examination boards have made changes in line with new developments. Full and short courses are offered. Controlled assessment has replaced coursework.

Edexcel's GCSE offers work on 'citizenship today'; 'participating in society'; 'citizenship in context' and 'citizenship campaign'. The campaign element of the course is principally aimed at those who take the full course but there are opportunities for active involvement in the short course. More details may be seen at www.edexcel.com/quals/gcse/gcse09/citizenship-studies/Pages/default.aspx. The resources on the Edexcel web pages are easy to navigate and provide many useful details including exemplar teaching, learning and assessment resources. I particularly recommend the PowerPoint on this page which gives a very clear overview of the requirements. Edexcel works closely with Pearson (Heinemann) and recommends a text on citizenship by Anthony Batchelor, Gareth Davies, Trevor Green and Pauline Standen.

OCR offers units on 'rights and responsibilities' and 'identity, democracy and justice'. For the full course, both of these themes are used but with suitably expanded commitments. The work on rights and responsibilities is sub titled 'extending knowledge and understanding' while the work on identity, democracy and justice is sub titled 'leading the way'. Full details are given at www.ocr.org.uk/qualifications/type/gcse/hss/citizenship_studies/index.html. Various resources are available with new texts being published by Hodder and written by authors including Tony Thorpe and Julie Nakhimoff.

AQA GCSE focuses on three topics: 'school, work and the local community'; 'national and European citizenship' and 'global citizenship' with three themes of 'rights and responsibilities'; 'decision making, power and authority' and 'participation in citizenship activities'.

Students will enjoy and le
citizenship activity that is
very many guides available
part in a practical project t
understanding but also allo
making a real contribution
encourage students to work

1. Getting started. Initial th
discussed in which the stu
questions: who should I w
should I work on?; what is
established (research and/
2. A planning phase in which
key steps that need to be ta
successful project. This wil
individually or in groups to
in relation to jobs and, imp
contingency plans at each st
questions need to be addres
played by each person in the
person have achieved by spec
are needed? Whose permissio
do we do if things go wrong?
explicitly considered at this p
ask these questions and shoul
respondents anonymity?). It is
consider at this stage practical
to be contact between the stud
3. Carrying out the project. If the
taken place carefully and thoro
crossed) the project itself shoul
4. Evaluating the project. It is imp
that evaluation should not be un
minute activity but rather shoulc
very beginning. Students need to
question that I am addressing?; w
do I intend to gather?; how will I
(e.g. statistical analysis of questio

re
m
a

The
that
of l
data
or w
a sp

IDEA

108

Encouraging GCSE Students to Make Good Presentations

Developing good presentation skills is a key element of citizenship education. The presentation of written work should, of course, follow the normal conventions associated with good standards of literacy but students can also be guided in ways that will allow for a very professional written presentation. The following is a guide to what should be written:

1. Introduction: by the end of the introduction the reader must be clear about the following: what is the argument made in this piece of work (it can be useful if the work begins 'as a result of doing this project I argue . . .'; what is the context for this study (why is it important); what was done during the project; what issues are discussed and what conclusions are drawn. (For example: 'As a result of doing this project I argue that the media sees young people as a threat but most are law abiding. During January–March 2010 significant reservations were raised through the media about the criminal activities of young people. I reviewed a wide range of media reports and then interviewed young people. I analyzed issues regarding petty and serious crime. I conclude that young people are generally law abiding and concerned to do well within existing society').
2. Context: what are the big ideas and issues that have led to the development of this piece of work?
3. Methods: what has been done in order to gather data; who formed the sample; what sort of data was used (interviews/questionnaires/news reports, etc.); what safeguards were put in place (was data only collected from certain people at specific times of the day and has all data been treated anonymously?).
4. Issues: what are the key arguments that are being made? (Normally, it would be useful if students could discus two or three arguments).
5. Conclusions and recommendations: what are the key final points that can be made and what suggestions are made for the future?

IDEA 109

Post 16 Citizenship

There are very many programmes in vocational and non-vocational programmes that are directly relevant to citizenship. Perhaps the most direct link can be seen in social science AS and A level programmes as well as relatively new AS programmes in citizenship (see details on, for example the AQA web pages). Review the specifications and examination papers of those courses in order to ensure that you are engaged in the best work available for your students.

A good range of resources are shown at www.excellencegateway.org.uk/ citizenship and it is worth considering the particular opportunities that can be gained through BTEC programmes in, for example, policy related courses including public volunteering. As well as the usual routes for citizenship education (6th form or college councils, mock elections, research projects, etc.) it is worth exploring what can be done with young adults as opposed to children. For some citizenship education for 11–16 year olds will always be restricted because of the limited experience of students and the need to safeguard them and others when educational experiences are being planned. Not all young adults in 6th forms and further education colleges are quite at the stage of being able to benefit from the focus on real life single issues that involve them in resolving disputes with housing authorities, employers and others. However, there are benefits to be gained from the additional responsibility and maturity that can be expected from those older than 16, while still keeping within the limits of a formal education programme.

of course, reflect the learning outcomes and must be consistent with the National Curriculum.

There are three assessment objectives:

AO1 Recall, select and communicate their knowledge and understanding of citizenship concepts, issues and terminology (assessment weighting: 25–35 per cent).

AO2 Apply skills, knowledge and understanding when planning, taking and evaluating citizenship actions in a variety of contexts (assessment weighting: 40–50 per cent).

AO3 Analyze and evaluate issues and evidence including different viewpoints to construct reasoned arguments and draw conclusions (assessment weighting: 30–40 per cent).

GCSE specifications in citizenship studies must allocate a weighting of 40 per cent to external assessment and a weighting of 60 per cent to controlled assessment in the overall scheme of assessment.

IDEA 106

What is Offered by the Three Examination Boards?

All examination boards have made changes in line with new developments. Full and short courses are offered. Controlled assessment has replaced coursework.

Edexcel's GCSE offers work on 'citizenship today'; 'participating in society'; 'citizenship in context' and 'citizenship campaign'. The campaign element of the course is principally aimed at those who take the full course but there are opportunities for active involvement in the short course. More details may be seen at www.edexcel.com/quals/gcse/gcse09/citizenship-studies/Pages/default.aspx. The resources on the Edexcel web pages are easy to navigate and provide many useful details including exemplar teaching, learning and assessment resources. I particularly recommend the PowerPoint on this page which gives a very clear overview of the requirements. Edexcel works closely with Pearson (Heinemann) and recommends a text on citizenship by Anthony Batchelor, Gareth Davies, Trevor Green and Pauline Standen.

OCR offers units on 'rights and responsibilities' and 'identity, democracy and justice'. For the full course, both of these themes are used but with suitably expanded commitments. The work on rights and responsibilities is sub titled 'extending knowledge and understanding' while the work on identity, democracy and justice is sub titled 'leading the way'. Full details are given at www.ocr.org.uk/qualifications/type/gcse/hss/citizenship_studies/index.html. Various resources are available with new texts being published by Hodder and written by authors including Tony Thorpe and Julie Nakhimoff.

AQA GCSE focuses on three topics: 'school, work and the local community'; 'national and European citizenship' and 'global citizenship' with three themes of 'rights and responsibilities'; 'decision making, power and authority' and 'participation in citizenship activities'.

IDEA

107

Planning a GCSE Citizenship Activity

Students will enjoy and learn a great deal from the citizenship activity that is part of the GCSE. There are very many guides available to helping young people take part in a practical project that develops their own understanding but also allows for the possibility of making a real contribution to society. Many teachers encourage students to work in four key stages:

1. Getting started. Initial thoughts are generated and discussed in which the students ask three issues or questions: who should I work with?; what topic should I work on?; what is the type of project to be established (research and/or practical initiative)?
2. A planning phase in which the students outline the key steps that need to be taken in order to achieve a successful project. This will require students either individually or in groups to develop a clear timetable in relation to jobs and, importantly, a set of contingency plans at each stage. This means that five questions need to be addressed. What role must be played by each person in the team? What must each person have achieved by specific dates? What resources are needed? Whose permission should be asked? What do we do if things go wrong? Ethical issues should be explicitly considered at this point (e.g. is it right to ask these questions and should the students promise respondents anonymity?). It is also important to consider at this stage practical safety issues if there is to be contact between the students and others.
3. Carrying out the project. If the planning phase has taken place carefully and thoroughly then (fingers crossed) the project itself should run fairly smoothly.
4. Evaluating the project. It is important to emphasize that evaluation should not be undertaken as a last minute activity but rather should be built in from the very beginning. Students need to ask: what is the key question that I am addressing?; what sort of evidence do I intend to gather?; how will I analyse that evidence (e.g. statistical analysis of questionnaire responses or a

review of interview data); what sections do I expect my report to have (and, later in the exercise, what argument am I making?).

The content and focus of projects can vary from those that investigate transport issues using the perspectives of local residents, to international enquiries gathering data from school students in other parts of the country or world, to practical engagement that aims to achieve a specific outcome.

IDEA

108

Encouraging GCSE Students to Make Good Presentations

Developing good presentation skills is a key element of citizenship education. The presentation of written work should, of course, follow the normal conventions associated with good standards of literacy but students can also be guided in ways that will allow for a very professional written presentation. The following is a guide to what should be written:

1. Introduction: by the end of the introduction the reader must be clear about the following: what is the argument made in this piece of work (it can be useful if the work begins 'as a result of doing this project I argue . . .'; what is the context for this study (why is it important); what was done during the project; what issues are discussed and what conclusions are drawn. (For example: 'As a result of doing this project I argue that the media sees young people as a threat but most are law abiding. During January–March 2010 significant reservations were raised through the media about the criminal activities of young people. I reviewed a wide range of media reports and then interviewed young people. I analyzed issues regarding petty and serious crime. I conclude that young people are generally law abiding and concerned to do well within existing society').
2. Context: what are the big ideas and issues that have led to the development of this piece of work?
3. Methods: what has been done in order to gather data; who formed the sample; what sort of data was used (interviews/questionnaires/news reports, etc.); what safeguards were put in place (was data only collected from certain people at specific times of the day and has all data been treated anonymously?).
4. Issues: what are the key arguments that are being made? (Normally, it would be useful if students could discus two or three arguments).
5. Conclusions and recommendations: what are the key final points that can be made and what suggestions are made for the future?

IDEA

109

Post 16 Citizenship

There are very many programmes in vocational and non-vocational programmes that are directly relevant to citizenship. Perhaps the most direct link can be seen in social science AS and A level programmes as well as relatively new AS programmes in citizenship (see details on, for example the AQA web pages). Review the specifications and examination papers of those courses in order to ensure that you are engaged in the best work available for your students.

A good range of resources are shown at www.excellencegateway.org.uk/ citizenship and it is worth considering the particular opportunities that can be gained through BTEC programmes in, for example, policy related courses including public volunteering. As well as the usual routes for citizenship education (6th form or college councils, mock elections, research projects, etc.) it is worth exploring what can be done with young adults as opposed to children. For some citizenship education for 11–16 year olds will always be restricted because of the limited experience of students and the need to safeguard them and others when educational experiences are being planned. Not all young adults in 6th forms and further education colleges are quite at the stage of being able to benefit from the focus on real life single issues that involve them in resolving disputes with housing authorities, employers and others. However, there are benefits to be gained from the additional responsibility and maturity that can be expected from those older than 16, while still keeping within the limits of a formal education programme.

SECTION 14

Learning from Others

IDEA

110

Exploring the Work of Cross National Surveys

The following are some of the key research projects that help to show what is happening across the globe for citizenship and civic education:

1. CiVED (see www.iea.nl/cived.html)

    1) 5 year study (1994–2002)
    2) Phase 1 qualitative national case studies
    3) Phase 2 cognitive test + quantitative surveys
    4) Involving over 28 countries, 3,000 14-year-olds in each country (over 80,000 students), teachers and school leaders in each country

2. ICCS (see www.iea.nl/icces.html)

    1) 4 year study (2006–2010)
    2) Quantitative national context survey and quantitative cognitive test + surveys
    3) Involving over 38 countries, 3,000 14-year-olds in each country (over 110,000 students), teachers and school leaders in each country.

3. Smaller scale work includes the INCA study of 16 countries (this report is available free on the NFER web pages); a project involving five countries (see Fouts, J. and W. O. Lee, (2004), *Citizenship Education.* Hong Kong: University of Hong Kong Press); a European network Children's Identity and Citizenship in Europe Association (see www.cicea.eu/).

So, what do we now know as a result of this work? There is an international journal – *Citizenship Teaching and Learning* (www.intellectbooks.co.uk/journals/view-Journal,id=193/) which contains in volume 6 number 1, an excellent overview by Carole Hahn of developments in citizenship education in many different countries.

Much of the above international work has been done by David Kerr and part of his snapshot summary of findings is:

1. 14-year-olds have some (limited) understanding of democratic values
2. there is a positive correlation between students' civic knowledge and their participation in civic life as adults
3. there is scepticism among students about conventional forms of political engagement apart from voting
4. there is a move towards informal 'social movement' participation
5. schools have untapped potential to influence positively civic preparation
6. schools that model democratic values and practices are most effective in promoting civic knowledge and engagement
7. students with high levels of home literacy are more likely to intend to participate in political and civic activities.

IDEA

111

CELS (Citizenship Education Longitudinal Study)

CELS is the biggest and longest-running study about the impact of citizenship education anywhere in the world. The project was commissioned by the Department of Children, Schools and Families (DCSF), and started in 2001, when citizenship education became a compulsory subject for all schools in England. It will end in 2010 and involve over 816 schools and colleges 37,809 students; 2,626 teachers; 679 school leaders and133 college leaders.

The aim of CELS is to study the effects of the compulsory citizenship education curriculum on young people and schools in England, and answer key questions such as:

- what are the effects of citizenship education on the knowledge, skills and attitudes of young people?
- how is citizenship education being delivered in schools, and how are these different delivery methods shaping outcomes for students and schools?

The headline messages are:

Successes: students participate; schools provide clearer structures for citizenship education; discrete time slots are increasingly used; a more specialist and experienced cadre of CE teachers is gradually emerging in schools.

Challenges: teachers have little time to develop citizenship education; participation in real issues is difficult; some students confuse PSHE and citizenship; examples of weak leadership still exist; teaching and learning methods can be unimaginative; teachers need more confidence about particular topics (especially the economy, the EU and Parliament and Government).

CELS is a major landmark in citizenship education. I see it as a genuine attempt to help raise the status of citizenship education, to embed it into schools and, most important, to reflect and to develop recommendations that are evidence based. Educational policy making is often the result of political fashion or whim. CELS helps teachers, teacher trainers, policymakers and many others to know what has been done and to have a much clearer idea about what needs to be done. Whether policymaking is actually congruent with the rhetoric of evidence-based reform is still to be seen.

KEY TEXT:

Keating, A., Kerr, D., Lopes, J., Featherstone, G. and Benton, T. (2009), *Embedding Citizenship Education in Secondary Schools in England (2002–08), Citizenship Education Longitudinal Study Seventh Annual Report (DCSF Research Brief 172)*. London: DCSF (available online)

IDEA 112

EPPI (Evidence for Policy and Practice Information)

EPPI reviews develop conclusions as a result of closely examining a question through the analysis of relevant literature. Summaries of the reports are shown below:

1. A systematic review of the impact of citizenship education on the provision of schooling

What did we find?

- the quality of dialogue and discourse is central to learning in citizenship education
- teacher-pupil relationships need to be inclusive and respectful
- contextual knowledge can lead to citizenship engagement and action
- a coherent whole-school strategy, including a community-owned values framework, is key
- teachers need support to develop the appropriate professional skills

What are the implications?

- professional education requires the development of an appropriate set of values, a body of knowledge and professional skills
- genuine participation in the learning process by teachers and students requires school-based decision making
- citizenship education requires teachers to trust their own professional judgement
- citizenship education should be an intrinsic part of whole-school development planning
- citizenship education requires a focus on higher order critical and creative thinking skills

2. A systematic review of the impact of citizenship education on student learning and achievement

What did we find?

Citizenship education requires learner-centred teaching and meaningful curricula. Such pedagogy is characterized by a facilitative, conversational approach. It can improve students' communication skills, academic achievement and higher order cognitive and intellectual development. It can engage students to think about the meaning of their personal stories and experiences, and lead to a greater participation in lessons. It can create a cooperative learning environment and lead to more positive self-concept.

What are the implications?

- the findings imply the need for a radical review of the system and structure of schooling to incorporate citizenship education strategies
- teachers need to be supported to develop a more holistic, process-oriented pedagogy
- traditional authoritarian patterns of control are no longer appropriate
- curricular flexibility is necessary

KEY TEXT:

Deakin Crick R. et al. (2004), *A systematic review of the impact of citizenship education on the provision of schooling. Bristol, University of Bristol and citizED*

Deakin Crick R. et al. (2005), *A systematic review of the impact of citizenship education on student learning and achievement. Bristol, University of Bristol and citizED*

Both the above reports may be seen at http://eppi.ioe.ac.uk/cms/Default.aspx?tabid=61

IDEA

113

Australia and Citizenship Education

In the 1990s, Australia began to address concerns about low levels of political knowledge and engagement by establishing high profile groups to consider the nature of civic education. It was decided to introduce *Discovering Democracy (DD)*. The provision of curriculum resources and support for teachers was at the heart of this $32 million dollar initiative. Resources were distributed free to all of Australia's 10,000 schools. These resources are still available and teachers may wish to compare textbooks with what is available in England. There was also an extensive programme of professional development. A range of targets characterized *Discovering Democracy* including knowledge, personal character traits and, very importantly, a set of values (tolerance, respect for others, freedom of religion and association).

DD was welcomed by many. There were also sharp disagreements involving a wide range of people (some of who supported the development of citizenship education and some who were opposed to it in principle). Debates have focused around the following:

1. Is DD an example of inappropriate centralized power over the federal states;
2. Does adding DD lead to an overcrowded curriculum;
3. Was DD given a particular political orientation by the then government (for most of the period in which it was being developed the Prime Minister was John Howard who was often at the centre of controversial policy developments);
4. Was there an appropriate programme of professional development? By 2003 nearly a third of teachers had minimal awareness of DD and it was claimed that teaching methods continued to be traditional;
5. The impact on students is still being investigated (recent work completed by Suzanne Mellor of the Australian Council for Educational Research) makes some very positive remarks about the power of citizenship education to help young people develop understanding and skills.

KEY TEXT:

Print, M. (2008), 'Education for Democratic Citizenship in Australia', in J. Arthur, I. Davies and C. Hahn (eds) *Education for Citizenship and Democracy*. London: Sage.

IDEA

114

Canada and Citizenship Education

Education in Canada is organized along provincial lines and so it is not possible to describe a simple, unified position about citizenship education that applies to the whole country.

Canada is now beyond the scare stories of the 1970s and 1980s that led some to suggest that the country would not survive the pressures associated with differences between the French and English speaking communities. But there have been (as in other countries) alarmist stories about low levels of young people's knowledge and engagement. This has led to calls for citizenship education and there have been developments in many provinces including British Columbia, Alberta and Ontario. The Citizenship Education Research Network (CERN) is a national organization that explores the nature of citizenship education.

In Ontario, civics was introduced in September 2000 as a compulsory half-credit course to be taken in grade ten (secondary school). The broad purpose is described as that which allows young people to develop their understanding following separate history and geography courses (each worth two credits). The province has declared that:

> The Grade 10 Civics course rounds out students' understanding of the individual's role in society by teaching them the fundamental principles of democracy and responsible citizenship. (Ministry of Education and Training 1999, 3)

The course:

> Explores what it means to be an informed, participating citizen in a democratic society. Students will learn about the elements of democracy and the meaning of democratic citizenship in local, national and global contexts. In addition, students will learn about social change, examine decision-making processes in Canada, explore their own and others'

> beliefs and perspectives on civics questions, and learn how to think and act critically and creatively about public issues. (Ministry of Education 1999, 47)

The Ontario curriculum guidelines make clear three key strands of the civics course: informed citizenship; purposeful citizenship and active citizenship. A variety of support mechanisms are in place for teachers including textbooks. There is little evaluation data available regarding the implementation of the new programme.

KEY TEXT:

Evans, M. et al. (2000), *Civics: issues and action*. Toronto: Prentice Hall.

Sears, A. and Hughes, A. S. (2008), 'The struggle for citizenship education in Canada: the centre cannot hold', in J. Arthur, I. Davies and C. Hahn (eds) *Education for Citizenship and Democracy*. London: Sage.

IDEA 115

Japan and Citizenship Education

Japan has been preparing young people for involvement in contemporary society for many years. But ideas about citizenship education in East Asia can be rather different from those in Europe, North America and Australia.

The history of civic education in Japan is entangled with wider political, cultural and demographic developments. The Imperial Rescript on Education in 1890 was the vehicle for nationalist and patriotic education. Confucianism is vitally important. This stresses social harmony, hierarchical relationships based on age and employment or community role, the importance of the family and concern for the less well off.

With a declining birth rate and more than 30 per cent of the population likely to be over 60 by 2050, the United Nations estimated in 2001 that to maintain the present workforce, 33.5 million immigrants will be needed. This has led to recognition by some that the old reliance on traditional ideas about nationhood and the supposed homogeneity of the Japanese will no longer do.

But there is a struggle taking place over the form of citizenship education that will emerge. In 2006 the Fundamental Law on education was revised. This emphasises community spirit, leading to independent participation in building society, together with the development of an attitude of wanting to contribute to its growth. In 1999 a law was passed which insists on the promotion of national symbols in schools. Different regions within Japan are developing very different approaches to citizenship education. In Shinagawa ward in Tokyo, programmes seem to emphasize respect for authority. Generally, students in Japanese schools have much more responsibility than schools in England and there are opportunities for mature and effective engagement.

It will be fascinating to watch how things develop over the next decade.

KEY TEXT:

Parmenter, L., Mizuyama, M. & Taniguchi, K. (2008) Citizenship education in Japan. Pp. 205–14 in J. Arthur, I. Davies and C. Hah (eds) *The Sage Handbook of Education for Citizenship and Democracy*. London, Sage.

SECTION

15

Professional Development

IDEA

116

Standards are clearly outlined (see www.tda.gov.uk/teachers/professionalstandards/standards.aspx). But, what do these mean for citizenship teachers and professional values? It is possible that schools and teachers have become both more to use a very broad brush description 'progressive' or 'liberal' in their use of language, dress codes, and general expectations of young people, and, at the same time, in their pursuit of academic qualifications and adherence to centralized policies more 'conservative'.

Ask teachers to think of three communities (e.g. the press and other media; parents; teachers of a subject other than citizenship) and their reaction to the following scenario:

A trainee teacher is with an English class. A project has been organized on the nature of language. A serious point about the use of language in different communities is being developed. Your colleague is showing a class the afternoon's TV coverage of the 3.30 p.m. horse race from Newmarket in order to analyze the language of the commentator, the bookmakers and the riders and owners. This is being done prior to an exploration of the sort of specialist language used by politicians. The head teacher unexpectedly brings a visitor to the classroom. The visitor is considering enrolling his child into the school. What reactions would you expect different communities to have to this situation? Has anyone acted unprofessionally: if so, who, how and why?

A simpler activity would be to consider a list of key behaviours (dress, speech, arrival time, presentation of written work, prompt achievement of tasks, communication with colleagues, etc.) and to suggest what would be regarded as professional behaviour in each context. It would be very important for time to be spent discussing the reasons why certain judgements are being made in certain contexts in order to avoid simple assertions. Is it normally the case, for example that citizenship teachers are more casually dressed than others in the staff room? If so, does this matter? Are teachers expressing political views and if so how? Certain types of clothing are now banned in schools in France: is this justified? Should we ban the wearing of wedding rings given it can be viewed as an assertion of sexual identity?

IDEA

117

- **Review the demands relating to subject knowledge made by various government agencies.** What does the DfE, Ofqual, Ofsted and others expect of students?
- **Review demands on subject knowledge associated with examination boards.** What are the similarities and differences between AQA, Edexcel and OCR for citizenship? It will be important to review examination papers, mark schemes and additional guidance to markers.
- **Create subject knowledge media folders.** Develop media folders classifying stories that relate to different areas of subject knowledge with notes for how these relate to intended learning outcomes. It is always important to focus on these learning outcomes rather than just look for a series of issue based exciting stories that may in the long run result in fragmented understanding of citizenship.
- **Encourage collaboration between colleagues so knowledge can be shared.** Useful conversations can take place with colleagues in history, geography, science, etc. Their subject associations will provide guidance on citizenship that you might find useful. But, again, your focus must be on citizenship; they will be looking for perspectives to support their own subject.
- **Review published material.** If you can be accepted as a reviewer of books or of articles for a journal this will be interesting and enjoyable but also ensure that you are kept up to date.
- **Establish regular subject knowledge reviews.** Once each year look again at your citizenship syllabus and ask yourself what sort of knowledge have you covered and what, in light of recent developments, now needs updating.
- **What new reading is available?** In the review sections of magazines such as *Prospect, New Statesman, Spectator, New Yorker, Times Literary Supplement,* etc. new material is summarized and one can easily and enjoyably learn about contemporary issues.

Consider the following simple flow diagram:

1. establish aim
2. undertake teaching activity
3. assess school students
4. establish new aim

Now consider a real lesson. Can the features shown above be identified or not? If so, were those features used in the planning process in the same order as shown above? Think about whether each of those elements could be used as a starting point. For example, an activity is generated not because it has a clear aim but rather because it is thought to be an interesting and enjoyable thing to do; start to work out if that could have a set of educational aims attached to it and what sort of assessment would be required. Now go further and question whether for citizenship the use of these features can ever be appropriate.

For some, citizenship is not to be taught in the same way as other lessons. It is possible to argue, by those who believe that citizenship is not the same as other subjects) that aims and assessment exercises are not to be considered at all when lessons are being planned. In other words, some feel that citizenship must allow for opportunities to explore what students think and to develop their capacity to become involved. What do you think?

My view is that we have to take seriously the findings of research that shows that discussions which are reasonably open lead to more effective learning. But it is very important not to allow for so much flexibility that the teacher is not guiding a learning process. I have seen lessons in which so many topics were introduced in such a 'lively' discussion that no one learned anything (other than perhaps that citizenship education was a frustrating experience). There has to be a clear educational focus that is achieved through a dynamic learning experience. The most vital part of what is planned is related to what students understand and what they can do. This often means identifying a concept (such as equality), developing a question about it (which requires investigation and analysis as well as more active involvement in the form of presentations, etc.), and teaching appropriately for that topic (e.g. in ways that allow for equal engagement by all students). The plan for this would not need to be developed sequentially in the way that is outlined at the top of this page.

A vast amount of material already exists to help teachers consider what needs to be done to manage classes and individuals effectively and appropriately. Citizenship, however, is thought by many to be more concerned with process than almost any other subject. The ways in which a teacher interacts with the class (as they promote a specific form of 'classroom climate') is said by some (see the reviews of research provided elsewhere in this book) to be a key feature of the citizenship teachers' work. What do you think about the sort of teacher behaviour shown below? Consider not just whether the teacher is an effective manager but, more precisely, what the class will be learning about citizenship if the teacher acts in this way:

A teacher stands very close to a student who is seated. There is direct eye contact. Explanations are being given by the teacher. The teacher makes a chopping motion with his hand as each point is made. [Possible response: the teacher is in charge; the student has to listen as the expert gives clear knowledge. There is a clear hierarchy in the class].

A teacher stands next to the whiteboard while talking to the whole class. The teacher leans back to hold the edge of the board, moves from foot to foot, and occasionally fiddles with the buttons on their jumper and with a pen. [Possible response: the teacher is unable to control the situation; is unsure and the class is being invited to seize power. This is not a democratic environment].

A teacher goes to a school student who is seated at a desk. The teacher leans down by bending their knees. Eye contact takes place occasionally. Nodding occurs when the student speaks. [Possible response: some suggest that this shows an attempt by the teacher at collaboration; it could be simply manipulative but there is an attempt to share power].

The NFER report on assessment in citizenship education (see www.nfer.ac.uk/nfer/publications/PCE01/PCE01summary.pdf) refers to the following challenges:

1. rationale and definition
2. scope and scale
3. consistency and progression
4. training and development
5. evaluation and review
6. sharing and dissemination.

The following outline could be discussed by teachers who want to assess a student's understanding of toleration. The teachers are presented with the following levels of response:

1. Students operating at a low level of toleration will simply be uninterested in the debates about citizenship.
2. Students who are disinterested are operating at a slightly higher level. Students see that there are different perspectives.
3. Students take a more careful interest in the exploration of a variety of standpoints. They explore who has said what; where they have 'come from'; what is in their interest and who will oppose them. Students may recognize conflicts between rights and freedoms.
4. Students consider a variety of perspectives in relation to limits to acceptable thinking and action and relate those ideas to principles of justice, rights and freedoms.

The following dilemmas could then be explored:

1. What does a student need to do to show that they are at a particular level? If, for example, a statement were made aggressively, would that conflict with the level of understanding about toleration?
2. What level of detail is needed? If, for example, a student said, when reflecting on a riot in a northern

English city that 'the police are rubbish', we would not want to accept that statement without knowing a good deal more about the thinking that lay behind it.

3. There is possibly a qualitative difference between statements three and four that is greater than the difference between levels two and three. Should levels be equidistant or are there are platforms from which further slight gains may be made by some?